# Transformative Path

## 7 Steps To Personal Growth And Empowerment

Parveen Smith

DEFINING MOMENTS PRESS

# Contents

# FREE GIFT

You are gifted a 7 Questions for Emotional Check In. How to check what you feel, to begin to transform your life. The link is here  Book | Soul 2 Soul (soul2soulwellbeing.com)

Parveen is also the author of two holistic books. Her true stories and Seeing Is Believing, Believing is Seeing and Head In Heaven Feet On Earth.

**Transform Your Life With Parveen Home | Soul 2 Soul Wellbeing**

*Want More Direction In Life?*

*Parveen is a transformative life coach, transforming lives daily.*

*She knows the paramount importance of health and wellbeing.*

*Prestigious Global Award Winner 2023*

*Award Winner Health & Wellbeing Champion 2024 New York*

*Global Speaker / Coach / Trainer*

**Get Your Free Gift!**

To get the best experience with this book, grab Parveen's 7 Questions For Emotional Check-in as a way to implement some tips to make your process transformative.

**You can get your 7 Questions by visiting:**

**Book | Soul 2 Soul (soul2soulwellbeing.com)**

# Acknowledgements

A big thank you to Lyn, Angela, Elaine, Chris, Nirmal, Sunny, Les, Sophia, Nadja, Amaka, and Dave.

Thank you to all of my clients and their beautiful honest testimonials.

I thank my family especially my husband for his patience.

Thank you to my mother who understood why I needed to write this book.

# Dedication To All My Readers

*I wholeheartedly welcome your interest in my books. The long-awaited book has arrived. The reason for this book to arrive is that as a mentor and transformative coach I see so many people worried about life situations and struggles. As you read this book, you will find solace in knowing you are not alone.*

*I thank my husband and my entire family for their patience while I have been busy writing this book to get it in your hands.*

*I thank all my clients for all their growth and trusting in me.*

*Growth happens when there is pain.*

*The only thing people don't know is that support is available during struggles and to be coached by us your struggles will lessen in a transformative way.*

To Andrea
Enjoy the steps and keep transforming

*Enjoy The Read*

With love
Parleen

# Foreword

The topic of the book 'Transformative Path". speaks for itself, identifying steps one may take to bring about positive change.

Over the years books have proved a huge support for me at times when I was searching for answers and felt the need to bring about positive changes to my life. Many feel their life is 'lacking' and following the steps outlined in Parveen's book will bring about a change that leads to contentment. When content, one is at peace and happy with life. I have worked as a complementary/holistic therapist for over 30 years and know that self-love is always the first and most important step that will bring about positive and lasting change to one's life.

Parveen has given many years developing her practice. Through many years of self-healing, she has transformed her own life from wheelchair user in constant pain to well-being therapist/coach, global speaker with boundless energy to do what she loves. She now has a huge urge, a calling and commitment to support and encourage others to do the same.

*Lyn Harvey*

# Introduction

S o, you have found us!

This is your journey, your path. How can one transform their path?

Maybe the thought for some of you is how can I even start to transform my path.

Well, look no further as I will give you some insights. Most of these insights are my experiences and my understanding from over the years.

I have had many profound experiences and I wanted to share the knowledge, the first-hand experiences, and the tools that I have acquired.

Are you going through a painful period of growth? Is your transition making you feel anxious or stressed? Are you struggling to sleep at night? Do you worry about the unknown? Does your soul want more?

I wrote this book in the hope of sharing some of my life traumas and inspiring you to grow. When I was going through trauma, I had nowhere to turn. Who would understand me? I am of Indian and Malaysian origin. My backstory will leave you in awe of the challenges, trials, and tribulations I endured. Yes, I wondered, "Why me?" Over my lifetime of experiences, I decided to share with the world how I faced distressing times, how I overcame them, healed from traumas, and transformed my life. I continuously say that life is a healing journey, and we must take the path to transform rather than remain stagnant.

Many people have told me that, when I speak in public, it feels as if I have had 30 major traumas in one small body. Listeners are left awed by the strength and resilience I have within. This strength and resilience exist for a reason.

Everyone is on their personal journey; you may be ahead and already implementing some steps, or you may be just beginning to understand your path. It is all okay. This book may evoke thoughts and help bring deeper understanding or heal certain aspects of your life. I suggest that when reading this book, you take time out to breathe, understand the points of view, and take what resonates with you, as everyone is at different stages of comprehending certain aspects of this journey.

Over my decades of work, I have met many people who felt lost, stuck, stagnant, depressed, anxious, fearful, or low-spirited. These descriptions are only a few. I offer many solutions that people can apply to get their lives back on track. The guidance and support of a coach are the quickest and best ways to be free from limitations, pain, and feeling stuck in life. Transformative Path will equip you well.

As I speak globally, I love to share that I am a fine example of transformation from illness and disability to wellness, from severe trauma to survival. As a coach and mentor, I have decades of experience in this field of transformation, appearing on national and international television and newspapers, showcasing that health is paramount. I also had my very own worldwide radio station, and one of my dear listeners, Nirmal, said how much I motivated many as a radio presenter, teacher, writer, and speaker. My reach has been wide, yet it is easy to forget until someone reminds you.

One physical body to have as your vehicle.

One soul as the guiding light.

One mind as the consciousness.

This book is for you if you want to transform your life, learn some techniques, and reduce the pain in your life for a happier existence. Who wants to live in despair?

Eunice said, "Parveen has the brightest aura. We walked into the room, she came in, and the world was telling us that this person is special and quite amazing. It was validated by the experiences we had conversing with each other and the energy that she shared. If anyone wants to speak to Parveen, you will be the lucky one to do so."

Jonny said, "In very simple terms, what Parveen went through is triumph over extreme adversity. I don't know how she can still smile."

P B said, "She is like a beacon of light. Everywhere she goes, people feel drawn to her. She automatically has the presence to transform something in a person. Many say they experience a shift in their life when they meet her."

I know how I can transform your life. It is incredible when you are on the right path, one that transforms you from your very core. Waiting is procrastinating something that will always stay the same. So, take the plunge, read this book, and get the best help to grow and empower yourself.

No more waiting for the right time—there is no right time.

The time is now.

Make yourself comfortable, as the time you share with me is going to be precious. This is an informative guide to your path!

If I can do it, so can you. Any pain is horrid to go through, whether it is physical, mental, or emotional. Oh, not forgetting the soul's pain. Yes, that is also you.

Suffer? Why should we? These days we have more knowledge and wisdom that can help us with the right tools. Some may say, "I'm not lost in life," but how do you know you aren't when you haven't dug deep into yourself? Many people carry on trundling along, doing the same old things, being the same old way, just scraping by to be happy.

Your happiness is everything because that is what the soul wants—joy too, and it isn't always materialistic happiness. However, who said you can't have it all?

Life was tough growing up; I am not going to lie about it. My anxieties started at a very young age—around three or four years old. My parents split up after many disagreements, most of which were probably because my mother kept having girls, and a boy was needed to carry on the surname. Then more traumas came, like being chased by neighbours' dogs to our primary school, where we literally ran for our lives crying. These dogs were purposely set to chase us by neighbours shouting out to the dogs, "Go and get the Pakis." This happened every day going to school and coming back. It was only us girls walking on our own as my mother had to look after the younger ones. Can you see how scared we were, running for our lives daily? That daily fear of going to school, knowing what was waiting for us—a dog set on us—was very frightening and scarred me for life.

Going out to get the family shopping was another ordeal. As my mother was a single parent with five girls, we only had a certain amount of money for the week's necessities. Many times, we had to put things back at the till as we didn't have enough money. Occasionally, someone would pay the extra amount as we held up the queue. Please allow me to tell you, this was no one's fault—it was just what it was. The only thing this did was make us feel embarrassed. For the weekly shop, we had to be smarter and make a list, guessing the price of each item to round it off. Funnily enough, we still got it wrong most times, of course, because we were only young children.

Then another trauma hit when I was fifteen. I missed a couple of my exams because I went to work in a factory to help the family out. I felt so stupid as I was told I would have to resit at college. I was almost a year behind my friends. The imposter syndrome of not being good enough started here. I was quite a shy girl growing up, and most of the time, I found my freedom walking for miles to get to college and back. During this time, I realised people hardly smiled at one another. I used to purposely make a point of eye contact and smile at everyone walking by. The freedom of fresh air, along with smiling, was a beautiful thing.

At the age of 17, the next trauma hit when I was forced into an arranged marriage. That was quite traumatic, but that is a whole new book! The reason I am sharing these episodes with you is so you can get an idea that when something happens, you can get through it.

During this period, as I was forced to live with people I didn't know, I was made to eat some black tar-like poison. I begged the person not to do this, but this person force-fed me, literally spooning the tar into my mouth, and making me swallow it. It was to abort my first baby.

Then at the age of 19, my sister was found dead. She never turned up at the corner of the street where we always met to walk to work together. We had many good conversations, and she revealed some of her life situations to me, but I didn't do anything about it. When she died, I lived with this guilt for a long time. My whole world had turned upside down!

At this stage, I felt it should have been me who died, not her. The guilt, pain, and hurt I felt were incredibly sad. I suffered from severe panic attacks, which were beyond anxiety and stress. This grief lasted with me for eight years, and the panic attacks and anxiety lasted decades.

As a summary of some of my early traumas up to my early twenties, I want to share this so you can see you are not alone. You may have had different things happening in your life, such as troubles with parents, not bonding, problems with marriage, dynamic family problems, loss of a loved one, moving home, an ill family member, looking after someone who is disabled, looking after an elderly parent, loss of earnings, or a change of career. The list is endless. As I say, there is so much that can be resolved or healed to help you transform your life. The knowledge in this book will bring many realisations.

As an expert in my field, supporting and transforming lives from anxiety, stress, depression, or feeling stuck in life is a privilege, as I have experienced this myself wholeheartedly. I trained as a mentor for schools over twenty years ago. I understand emotions and adversity. Working with thousands of people, whether speaking globally, presenting workshops, coaching, mentoring, or training people, has been my longest passion in life. I am truly privileged to be alive, healthy, and well. This is my true vocation in life.

This is why I say you don't need to suffer, as there is support and a service for all.

Within the chapters that follow, you will find 7 steps to embrace change, 7 steps to personal growth and empowerment. There will be subheadings as we enter different subject matters. Within each chapter, there are 7 tools you can apply.

We will outline symptoms and scenarios, and then you can keep notes in your special books or journals of the transformations you desire and use the tools provided. There will be questions you can answer in your own time as you go through this book. You will gain awareness of things that have either happened in your life or are currently happening. You may encounter light bulb moments. So, reflection may be required after each chapter or as you go along with each subheading.

*"The first step toward change is awareness. The second step is acceptance." - Nathaniel Branden*

# CHAPTER ONE

# Step One

## WHAT IS TRANSFORMATION?

What is transformation? Transformation is change. For some, it may be a dramatic change, and it can take various forms. For example, it could be a personality change, a change in a person's character, or something like a seed growing into a flower. For me, transformation is all about change in a way of being, meaning a change in perspective, behaviour, or mindset. Transformation can also be physical, involving the body. Transformation is a process, like an alchemical change, taking something basic and turning it into something great, like wrought iron into gold. Transformation, in my understanding, is growth—improving something in your life, mind, emotions, physical being, or mental wellness. We are all evolving every single day because we are human beings and living beings.

Change takes time. Change can be natural. We have all evolved over many years, in fact, thousands of years. We are evolving from our parents and ancestors. For example, if our parents had a certain way of being, we may choose not to follow in their footsteps. We're changing something within us because we want that change. We may hear someone say, "I wouldn't like to be like my mother; she was so harsh bringing us up," or about their father. So, there is an inclination to change that behaviour or character within us. Their behaviours and values may not align with ours now. Our parents may have been influenced by their parents, and so forth. A lot of what we do and how we behave may be what we learned from our parents.

On the other hand, you may hear someone say, "Actually, I want to be just like my mum or dad because they brought me up in a perfectly loving way." This influence can be a positive one and of great value. Traits are part of evolution; we carry traits from our ancestors and generations, and these traits are passed down. In our realisations, we decide whether we like these traits or want to change them. Changing traits and behaviours from our ancestors helps our growth, and many of us want growth. Times are changing, and it's all evolution. There are many growth opportunities. Many people want diversity, transformation, and more emotional, mental, physical, and soulful growth. Once we realise certain patterns need change, limiting beliefs are easier to overcome.

As we know, times have changed since the 1900s. Times have changed from mandatory labour work to the machine and digital revolution. The evolution of the mind, even just thinking about it, is unbelievably complex. Our human brain has changed and expanded into higher thinking. Human behaviour has evolved, and our decision-making, problem-solving, and innovative ideas show the changes in the mind. We are computing things that we would never have thought of 100 years ago. Evolutionary growth is fast and vast, especially in the digital world. The digital growth from the past 100 years has been exponential. It's been unprecedented and transformative. I remember when I started using technology in the 1980s. I was so excited that computers were available to some families, and they were huge machines that seem so ancient now. The world then was so different from what we see now. We had limited electricity around the world, limited telephone, and communications. Now we see the world computing differently, in an advanced manner. Gone are the handwritten letters and telegrams, except for the digital telegram. Newspapers are still around but minimal. Many people still like to hold books in their hands, but we have digital books as well. There is so much growth in the world. The Internet has been very advantageous for all of us because we have had growth. The transformation is before our very eyes. We have connections with many parts of the world and can access information at our fingertips. Our social media platforms have grown. We are now living and working in such an unbelievable way that we would never have imagined 100 years ago. The whole world is being connected through the growth of the digital world. All ages and cultures are connected, and this has really shaped our societies in unimaginable ways.

## What is the purpose of life?

I know many people wonder, "What is the purpose of life?" What is the purpose of your life? How does this question make you feel? Do you know your purpose? What fills your heart with joy? What longings do you have that you would like to fulfil? Isn't it fascinating when we ask ourselves these questions?

The purpose of life is to enjoy, learn, and grow. It's that simple for me. But I know that for many people going through the most difficult times in life, it's not that simple. It is a journey. Everyone has a unique, individual journey. The destination is full of life and will reveal itself as the person embarks on the journey.

What desires do you have that you feel you want to fulfil? If you ask me what my purpose in life is, my purpose is very clear, and I've been blessed to be on this journey. Not everything came easily, trust me. But of course, every single person is different. Someone might see their purpose as being an office worker. Someone else might see their purpose as working in law. Others might see their purpose as being a police officer, a fireman, a nurse, or a doctor. Some may see their purpose in gardening, landscaping, or conservation, and this is also very meaningful.

Each person will have their own desires and personal fulfilment. Some people already know exactly what their purpose is, while many others are still searching and looking to find personal fulfilment. We learn, grow, and adapt. For some people in this lifetime, it may be that they just want to be happy, and they're quite content with minimal growth. They don't want much out of life, and that's fine too because that's their soul's path. That's their soul's journey. Remember, your purpose is uniquely yours and everything will start to evolve as your desires grow and you want more.

Those who are seeking happiness will find that it is actually a byproduct of being in our soul's purpose or being in our purpose. There is no right or wrong answer here. We just learn to evolve, adapt, and grow. For those willing to make these choices and take the steps, they will see their purpose. The purpose of life is a very personal question and a very personal answer.

From a personal point of view, I am much happier evolving rather than staying stagnant in life. Again, that's a very personal perspective.

Below are 7 thoughts that may help your transformation:

## The Purpose Of Life Thoughts

1. To find your way through the web of life

2. Remember everyone's journey is different

3. Karma is what you give out you will get back

4. Things will get better every day in every way

5. Our opinions are our own opinions be kind

6. The past cannot be changed. Let go and live on

7. The inner joy is the most important

*Nothing is lost, nothing is created, everything is transformed*
*Antoine Lavoisier*

# CHAPTER TWO

# Step Two

## ANXIETY, STRESS & DEPRESSION

D id you know that I suffered from anxiety for decades? I was going through so many continuous traumas that I didn't know what to do. I didn't even know what anxiety was, only that my body and mind were feeling things—yes, things I will call them—because as a child, you cannot put words to what is happening to your body and in your body. A few years after the death of my sister, I sought medical help.

### Anxiety, Stress And Depression

How many people suffer from anxiety and stress in the world we live in, and what is it costing people? Relationship problems, divorce, loss of jobs, loss of homes—the negative impact can be huge. Anxiety disorders are prevalent globally. The World Health Organisation estimates that around 264 million people suffer from anxiety disorders. The prevalence varies by region, culture, and socioeconomic factors. Anxiety and stress contribute to physical health issues such as cardiovascular problems, weakened immune systems, and digestive disorders. Anxiety can lead to depression, panic attacks, and other mental health conditions. Chronic stress strains relationships, leading to conflicts, communication breakdowns, and emotional distance. Just looking at how many people suffer or struggle with mental health problems is astounding—the figures change daily, I am sure. The impact on the physical body as well as the mind is huge, so this is the question: who is ready to feel healthier?

## Anxiety

So, let's look at what anxiety is. Anxiety is a natural response to stress. It can also occur in threatening situations, causing feelings of worry, fear, or unease. Everyone experiences different signs of anxiety, with varying levels from mild to severe. Anxiety can be triggered by certain situations, scenarios, or events. The levels of anxiety can vary, impacting a person's life on a daily, monthly, yearly, or even decades-long basis.

I have personally seen many people with anxiety who didn't even realise what it was. They didn't recognise that they had been experiencing anxiety for the last 20 years. Prolonged anxiety can definitely impact you mentally, emotionally, and physically. Let's look at some of the symptoms of anxiety.

- Difficulty in concentrating

- Irritable

- Body feeling tense

- Feeling shaky

- Trouble sleeping

- Pacing the room

- Fast heartbeat

- Sweating

Now, these are just some of the symptoms a person may feel during anxiety.

According to data from Mental Health UK, 6 in 100 people in the UK alone will be diagnosed with Generalised Anxiety Disorder. Over 8 million people are experiencing an anxiety disorder at any one time.

## Stress

Let's have a look at stress. Stress and anxiety actually go hand in hand. Stress is the body's natural response when a challenge presents itself and can affect the physical, mental, and emotional self. When stress levels are high, we must understand that something needs to change. Most of us can thrive on some level of stress, which helps us keep on track with projects or things we need to accomplish. However, excessive stress, especially when chronic, can be debilitating. The most common sources of stress include:

- Arranging a wedding

- Moving home

- Separation/ Divorce

- Death/bereavement

- Job interview

- Relationship problems

- Financial difficulties

So even in this category, where there is overlap with anxiety, you may experience irritability, tension in parts of the body, fatigue, headaches, and difficulty concentrating—just to name a few symptoms.

It's important to remember that when your anxiety and stress levels are very high, you may require medical support. Always contact your doctor or consultant, as each person's experience of symptoms can vary, necessitating expert advice.

According to the latest data from 2023, an estimated 822,000 workers are affected by work-related stress, depression, or anxiety every year, as reported by the Health and Safety Executive. Additionally, 13.7 million working days are lost each year in the UK due to work-related stress, anxiety, and depression, costing £28.3 billion annually (NICE data cited by Health Champion).

Out of all the employees in the UK workforce, only 10% seek mental health support, according to data from 1Stop4aGP. These statistics are expected to rise as more people struggle through life.

So, my question is: when do people really ask for help? When do they seek the support, they truly need?

## Depression

Let's look at depression. Depression can be quite serious and is also common. It is known as a serious mental health condition that profoundly affects how a person feels, perceives the world around them, thinks, and manages daily life. Depression goes beyond simply feeling sad or having a bad day—it's much more than that. Some people may experience a milder form of depression depending on its cause.

Now with depression, a person may experience the below:

- Depression can go into a different realm of severe sadness

- Continuous, persistent sadness

- Lack of self-worth

- Fatigue

- Tearful

- Extreme lethargy

- Lack of concentration

- Absolute hopelessness

- Extremely low mood

- They are withdrawn

- Cannot think properly

- They may not even smile

- Don't want to leave the house

- They may feel there is no purpose to life

- They may feel they can't even get out of bed

- They don't want to engage with anybody

- They are not doing the normal daily activities within the house

- They may have lost interest in the activities around them

- Loss of interest in friendships

- There could be changes in their appetite

- Eating more or eating less

- Thoughts of self-harm

- They may feel they have no will to live

- Suicidal thoughts

- Suicide attempts

Living with someone who has depression is also not easy. I have had conversations with people who shared how difficult it was, leading to the end of relationships due to the intensity of depression. There may be emotional outbursts, and you may often find yourself last on their list of priorities. Living with someone who has depression often requires sacrifices and is recognised as a challenging path. You may gain various perspectives that enter your consciousness, and you may find yourself in need of help as well. Can you see the ripple effect from one person struggling with depression and its impact on others?

Depression is a definite psychological factor. It may be linked to our environment or genetics. Regardless of the cause, it's crucial to recognise these symptoms and understand what depression looks like for different people. By understanding the cycles of depression, we can support those experiencing it or direct them to appropriate treatments. There are numerous options available for people suffering from depression. Seeking medical advice from a doctor is typically the first step, where they may recommend medication, lifestyle changes, or therapy. Once identified, it's essential to seek appropriate care. While some individuals can manage their depression independently, severe cases require professional support. I firmly believe that these concerns are primarily aimed at improving individuals' quality of life.

According to Mind Charity, 3 in 100 people have depression. Of course, these figures are continuously changing. The data is given at this time in June 2024.

I have had many conversations with Sophia, who has experienced severe depression, and she encourages people not to hide from it. Here's what she shared:

"**I am grateful for my life story, as I know it brings H.O.P.E. in more ways than one!** My story of survival of major d*pression and multiple suicide attempts may bring encouragement and hope to someone who may currently be suffering with this in their lives, whether afflicted by it directly, or indirectly by caregiving for someone who is going through it. I've been knocked down by it 4 times, and the last time around it led me to have to shut down my dream business and nearly end my life more times than I can count on my fingers and toes. *It doesn't have to be this way...* for me, or for ANYONE. And that's why now I've made it a point for

my story to bring **H.O.P.E. to humanity by Helping Open People's Eyes** so that we normalize the conversation and never let anyone suffer in silence ever again! The normalizing for me started a long time ago when I began to openly speak about the darkest moments of my life. And it went a step further when I decided to pour these darkest moments in my first book, "Mom, I HAVE A PROBLEM". By taking part in the normalizing of this conversation as well, you too can contribute to greater SOUL HEALTH worldwide."
Sophia Manarolis M. Ed

We often hear about people who have ended their lives due to the problems they were facing. Sometimes, the person didn't actually want to go through with attempting suicide, but sadly, it's often too late. This is what I have heard from people I have spoken to. Recognising signs is important, and sharing these signs with people who know the person can help.

Let's look at anxiety and panic attacks. When the body is overloaded with fear, worry, and apprehension, it can feel really awful. There seems to be no let-up during this period, and it can feel overwhelming and challenging to overcome. Panic and anxiety attacks can be highly disruptive to the person experiencing them.

## Anxiety attacks

Anxiety attacks are reactions to stressors, often caused by feelings of worry, apprehension, and unease.

Panic attacks can suddenly appear without warning, being very intense and filled with fear. They can occur without any specific trigger, overwhelming the person experiencing them.

What does it feel like to have a panic attack?

- Racing heart

- Shortness of breath

- Chest pains

- Dizziness

- Feels life threatening

I asked a psychologist these questions: What happens to a human being psychologically when they experience shock and trauma? Is the pain felt in the body real, or is it all in the mind?

Shock triggers the sympathetic nervous system, prioritising survival. Blood circulation shifts, muscles receive increased blood supply, and emotions and pain perception may be temporarily muted. This survival mode can persist, highlighting the importance of reconnecting with others post-accident to activate the social engagement system.

Trauma involves a form of separation, whether from emotions, physical sensations, or parts of the body, sometimes leading to mental dissociation or, in severe cases, multiple personalities.

During trauma, sensory modalities and channels may become disconnected. Pain, as an interaction between body and mind, includes a pain memory stored in patterns closely tied to affected body parts.

While pain is real, it can also be retained as a memory. The body may suppress immediate pain to cope, storing it as an association with past experiences.

Can these feelings subside? Yes, I believe these feelings can lessen over time, although the process can be unpredictable and may require medical support. Incorporating relaxation techniques can be beneficial. Here are some techniques I've found useful and encourage my clients to try:

## **Technique 1: Deep Breathing**

- -Sit down and take a deep breath in through your nose.

- -Hold your breath for 3 seconds.

- -Exhale slowly through your mouth.

- -Affirm to yourself that you are safe.

## **Technique 2: Recall Happy Moments**

- -Find a quiet place to sit.

- -Recall the happiest moment you've experienced.

- - Focus on that memory and feel it in your heart.

**Technique 3: Listen to Relaxing Music**

- - Even in a busy or public area, use your phone to find calming music.

- - Listen to the music while breathing gently.

**Technique 4: Lavender Oil**

- - Apply a lavender oil mixture to your pulse points (wrists and ankles).

**Technique 5: Use of Lavender Essential Oil**

- - Burn lavender essential oil in a burner.

- - Place lavender oil on your pillow for a calm night's sleep.

- - Practice gentle breathing while relaxing.

**Technique 6: Chamomile Tea and Environment**

- - Drink chamomile tea to promote calmness.

- - Reduce caffeine intake.

- - Sit and observe nature or a plant to soothe your mind.

## **'Technique 7: Gentle Walk**

- - Take a leisurely walk with a friend or family member.

- - If comfortable, engage in conversation during the walk.

- - Enjoy the peacefulness of a quiet stroll.

## **'Testimonial**

"I used Parveen's tools to help with my anxiety, and over time, I felt my body becoming calmer. Feeling safe was important to me, and these techniques really helped. I now regularly drink chamomile tea, which I've found soothing." - GC

These techniques are supportive in managing anxiety, stress, and depression day by day. Consider how your body and mind feel and see if these steps can be beneficial for you. Always seek medical help if needed.

*"Stress is caused by being 'here' but wanting to be 'there'." ~ Eckhart Tolle*

# CHAPTER THREE

# Step Three

## TYPES OF PEOPLE

### Empathic And Non-Empathic People

I wanted to share some thoughts about empathic and non-empathic people. I think it's important to understand how we can feel on our own journey of empowerment. I will start with empathic people. Below is a list of characteristics that empathic people embody. As you read them, you can connect with either the empathic list or the non-empathic list. We are all unique beings, and you may see a list that suits you. This will allow you to reflect on some aspects of your character and traits.

## Empathic People

- Sensitive to the energy of other people

- Good at reading people

- Compassionate and caring

- Warm-hearted naturally

- Emotionally Intelligent

- Strong intuition and trust it

- Good communicators and find the right words

So, just to elaborate: Empathic people are sensitive to energy. They are sensitive to the energy of other people, as well as to their emotions and feelings. These people can be described as very intuitive and compassionate. They are empathetic towards others, and they are better able to tune into other people's body language, tone of voice, and overall vibration. This enables them to pick up on the emotions and moods of the people around them. Empathic people usually need to take more care of themselves, and it's good for them to set boundaries to protect their own emotional well-being. Exercises like grounding yourself and setting healthy boundaries can be beneficial. If you are a sensitive person, you are easily affected by other people's emotions and how they feel, which can lead to becoming drained, overwhelmed, and even emotional yourself. For some people, being empathic on this level and feeling people's energy can be useful. At the same time, it can also be a hindrance if it affects you too

TRANSFORMATIVE PATH

much. Therefore, you should always prioritise your own emotional health to live a harmonious life.

To summarise, I think that empathic people are good at reading others; they can absorb their emotions and feelings like a sponge. People who are good at reading others are also good listeners. They are deeply caring, put their heart into everything they say or do, and can read into a person's every emotion. They are warm-hearted, natural people who are compassionate. They are also emotionally intelligent, have strong intuition, trust it wholeheartedly, and are gentle, loving communicators who can also be direct.

So now, please take a moment to reflect on the attributes above. Are any of those attributes YOU?

Take a moment and circle the ones that you feel describe you.

## Non-Empathic People

- Low emotional intelligence

- Poor communicators and cannot find the right words

- Struggle to understand others and only see their point of view

- Lack in empathy, now this is when you are not considerate, you may be classed as this

- Insensitive to the individual not thinking of their feelings

- Poor intuition is when they don't understand what intuition is

- Emotionally distant is more as though they are closed off

So, let's take a closer look at non-empathic people. These individuals can lack interest in the feelings of others and do not always understand them. They can also have difficulty empathising with others. Usually, non-empathic people tend to put their own needs first. In my professional career, I have seen people with non-empathic tendencies who consider themselves much more important than others, and it can appear that they are insensitive or rude because they place more importance on themselves. But these are just their character traits. These traits can affect everyone around them and all relationships, potentially changing the dynamics of a household or business, usually for the worse or as a challenge.

As much as we do not want to punish anybody in any way or form, if we look back in history, laws were there for a reason. Emotions can be linked to crimes committed for non-empathic reasons. Of course, right now, I'm talking about the extremes of non-empathic people. The karmic understanding is that when a person commits unnecessary crimes or takes harmful actions consciously towards another, there will be repercussions that always come back to the individual. Empathic people know that it's unfair, and they understand that there is no reason or necessity to take revenge. When there's a conflict between empathic and non-empathic people, through verbal conflict, and harm is caused, it is an experience. From that experience, it is best to learn and let go. Letting go of negative expressions makes room for growth and new positive experiences. I often see people holding onto verbal conflicts, which only blocks their personal growth. In some situations, we see murderers being forgiven by the victim's family. They may see it from a point of moving on and letting go. Often, families meet after such incidents to gain resolution through communication and empathy. This can serve both parties.

In my case, when we found my sister dead, it was the most horrific situation you could ever go through. There were no answers. We felt this was an impossible situation. When she was found dead, her 18-month-old daughter was in the same room as her. The questions were why, how could this happen, and it didn't make sense. Our whole world had just ended. The panic attacks started quite quickly, and there was complete jittering of the whole body. There was no place or person that could have made this better. No one! The trauma and the shock were too deep.

So now, I want to share: did I have empathy for the person I knew was involved with my sister? No. I had hatred for this person. I was angry. I was 19. I had just lost my best friend. I just knew in my heart he caused all this. I say this also because he was non-empathic. I apologise if this topic is traumatic, but if we do not talk about these things, who will? We cannot brush these subjects under the rug.

When we look at empathic and non-empathic people, there can be a wide gap in understanding. So, you can make your own decisions on how empathic you can be after a tragic event involving a non-empathic person.

Please take a moment to think about each of the above traits. Are any of them yours? Most of you reading this book, I feel, will be empathic. It may well be that you know someone who fits either list above.

Take a moment and circle the characteristics that you believe are yours. This is a good exercise as it can make you aware of your character and traits.

Can you see how anxiety, stress, depression, empathy, and non-empathy play roles in our lives? We must consider that many aspects of ourselves are either obstacles or growth.

I have always been empathic, and sometimes that was a hindrance because when I was overwhelmed with empathy, I became emotionally involved in other people's problems. I realised that sometimes I needed to detach myself from other people's emotional issues because they took me off my path of supporting the people who needed my help. It was also a loss in more than one way.

If you feel overwhelmed by any of the issues so far, please take a moment to breathe, make yourself a cup of tea, and remember that you are not alone.

Reflect on each chapter to assist your growth.

*"Learning to stand in somebody else's shoes, to see through their eyes, that's how peace begins. And it's up to you to make that happen. Empathy is a quality of character that can change the world." ~ Barack Obama*

# CHAPTER FOUR

# Step Four

## THE SOUL AND THE MIND

**What is the soul? Let's see how you perceive the soul.**

E veryone has their own idea of what the soul is. I will look at the subject from a different angle than that of religion. I am going to explore a more philosophical perspective to understand what I think the soul is. It is the essence of who you are. It is a part of you, your personality, the depth of your true signature, your identity, your compassion. Your soul is not the body. The body is the physical vehicle that carries your entire existence, allowing activities to take place as the mind controls the body. The soul is simply the essence of who you truly are on the inside. In my personal perception, the soul also contains eternal memories, wisdom, and an imprint. We bring this essence with us into every life.

## The Soul

The soul can be joyful, humble, loving, or struggling. It is imperative that we go deeper because you are here to read about the transformational path to make a difference, right? We have covered aspects of transformation, anxiety, stress, depression, and empathic and non-empathic people to show you how to further transform yourself and let go of some suffering you may be experiencing.

## What is the suffering of the soul?

The suffering of the soul can manifest as emotional or spiritual pain, which a person can experience on a deeper level. It can be due to past traumas, fears, anxieties, stress, and a feeling of emptiness. This feeling of having no purpose in life, no passion or desire, may extend to oneself and others. The suffering of the soul is often a result of inner turmoil, reflecting what the individual feels at a deep soul level. It can signify a crisis where the person questions the purpose of their existence and why their life feels devoid of meaning.

This deep questioning often happens when a person suffers at the soul level and feels lost, missing something within, or hasn't yet found themselves. It could be that they have not yet found their full purpose in life and feel unfulfilled. This is when the journey of self-discovery begins for most people. However, some people get stuck at this point because they do not know how to find themselves. In such cases, they need support from a life coach or someone who can understand their lost feelings and help them find the purpose of life and why they feel disconnected from themselves and others.

Self-discovery takes time and is not something that changes overnight. Well-being is paramount at this stage. A lost soul that doesn't know its purpose or direction can lead to depression and suicidal tendencies. The soul needs nurturing, and well-being is crucial. Many times, I have coached clients to reach their realisations, feel in control, and take inventory of their life.

"The most authentic thing about us is our capacity to create, to overcome, to endure, to transform, to love and to be greater than our suffering." - Ben Okri

## Journey Of The Soul

The journey of the soul in this life is to live a happy life of abundance, knowing that you were born to parents who had their own characteristics. Your realisations come to light regarding what you truly want—whether their traits or your own. The journey of the soul may involve connecting with nature and experiencing the fullness of creation around you: seeing the mountains, the sky, and all the elements, and hearing the sounds of nature. This can inspire us and remind us that we are alive.

The journey of the soul is to live in the most harmonious relationships, to find abundant happiness, to feel serene within, to live in balance, and to create your own destiny. Your true self resides in your soul. This is how the soul frees itself from suffering. The soul wants to be content, not only with the inner self but also with the outer environment, as it mirrors the soul.

In this materialistic world, the soul understands that money makes the world go round; it pays our bills, puts food on our table, and provides us with a roof over our heads. The material world can be glamorous and ambitious. But when you have tried many ways to find happiness in the materialistic world and it does not bring you joy, you know you need to return to the basics of your soul. Negative experiences or challenges can transform into a deeper understanding of higher consciousness. When we are in tune with our soul through deep sufferings, we realise that we are indeed wise.

There may have been many paths before us, with twists and turns, different paths and roads we have had to travel because we did not understand what the soul truly wanted. I want to share with you that we can have it both ways when we are in balance and in tune with our soul's path. We can live in balance in the materialistic world and be more in tune with the soul. Those who have walked many paths of turbulence, uncertainty, and pain may realise that the soul has always wanted love, peace, and contentment.

## The Mind

The mind is very powerful, and we must learn to control it. It is a powerful tool, but it does not easily let go of questions and problems. Our mind can either keep us stuck or move us forward, helping us achieve and accomplish things. It can compare, analyse, and judge, and it can dwell in the past or the future. However, the present moment is the only moment of true existence, as it can never be repeated. The exact same experience can never be had again. For some people, the mind feels like a never-ending treadmill, with racing thoughts overtaking their existence.

Our minds can become overwhelmed, whether by work or personal situations, and we know that we can have thousands of thoughts a day. When does our mind truly rest? You might think it rests when you sleep, but the mind is always thinking about something. When is it ever in pure silence? Despite this, the mind is very powerful and helps us navigate the world we live in. Therefore, we need to learn to control ourselves and our minds, using them to our advantage. We use our mind to help us focus and achieve our goals, and we keep it calm to maintain the best relationships. This allows us to be what we want to be in the ever-changing business and materialistic world.

When we search for our true identity, we connect to the soul, which is our true essence. The heart is a part of this process, enabling us to continue enjoying the world we live in, understanding its limits and expense. While the materialistic world plays a role, the discovery of the soul and the understanding of how the mind works are much more powerful.

Living in fear is a huge challenge and a stopper of growth. Fear keeps you bound, like a brick wall that you cannot climb over. It is like drowning. I have experienced many situations in my life where I have been held down by fear, to the point of not being able to move. After my third baby, when my pelvis split during childbirth, I had the most horrendous experience of my life. What should have been a joyful, albeit painful, experience became a living nightmare. I endured the inability to walk during pregnancy and afterward. Being in acute pain became my label. It wasn't the fear of disability I am talking about, but the fear of movement. This fear was with me day and night for four and a half years. I feared that if I moved, I would break and not be able to be put back together again.

I remember, a couple of years down the line, when I could sit up, I tried to move a few inches away from my original place. I was terrified. The fear paralysed me, even though I was already paralysed with pain. That movement to sit a few inches to the side of the sofa was literally terrifying.

My husband got the book "Feel The Fear And Do It Anyway." At the time, I could barely read due to blurred vision, but when I did read it, it made sense.

Your soul is eternal, and it will be eternally grateful to know that you understand it, not just your personality. I see an aspect of the personality as you, the part that operates daily with your name, identity, and character. This part of your personality is an everyday function. Your soul, however, is beautiful and seeks contentment, balance, and unconditional love.

When an individual reaches a certain point in life, the soul becomes the observer, witnessing everything in front of you. The soul is you. As you grow, develop, and become wiser, you will witness beyond the personality what your life truly is. My perspective on the eternal nature of the soul is quite profound. It's fascinating to consider the interplay between our personality and the deeper essence of our being. I describe the soul as an observer beyond the everyday functions of our personality, resonating with wisdom and introspection. Indeed, as we evolve and gain experience, our awareness expands beyond the confines of our immediate identity. The soul, in its timeless existence, seeks contentment, balance, and unconditional love. It yearns for a harmonious alignment with the universe.

Over time, I pondered many things about the soul and the purpose of its eternal essence. I realised that when the soul is awakened to observing, the personality can become the best version of itself. Every emotion, action, and behaviour will bring out a different character, which I see as the best version of you.

I realised a few decades ago that my thoughts control my outcomes, but I still needed to learn more about these concepts.

You are such a powerful human being and just don't know it. You have the 6th sense of incredible intuition. Little do you know how you can use it to your benefit.

No one hurts you; you feel hurt.

No one stops you from doing anything; only you do.

Negative thoughts equal negative outcomes.

Positive thoughts equal positive outcomes.

These realisations kept coming to me. I processed them internally and lived by these values as much as I could.

## There are 7 soul and mind thoughts below that you can participate in.

1. How do you perceive your soul?

2. How do you see your soul, joyous or struggling?

3. Are you ready to go deeper to explore more about you?

4. Are you achieving your soul's desire?

5. Does your mind run away with thoughts?

6. Would you like to have more peace of mind?

7. Now take 3 minutes close your eyes and gently breathe.

You have already taken the time to absorb the information and will discover more about yourself and maybe the people around you. I am so impressed that you have come this far and are applying some of the concepts from the book. Never give up, because your mind and soul are incredibly powerful. I just wanted to remind you of this. You may also want to consider my wellness sessions, which are highly transformative.

## **'Testimonial**

It's heartbreaking to see your teenage daughter suffering so much with crippling anxiety, especially having tried many remedies and techniques, all of which failed to help, until we met Parveen. In just one session, my daughter felt lighter, her head was clearer and most of all her anxiety had improved tenfold. Parveen is quite honestly a miracle worker. After three sessions my daughter felt happier, calmer and more able to deal with life's challenges. We are so thankful to Parveen; she truly is an angel.
*Laura Capewell*

"A man is but the product of his thoughts, what he thinks, he becomes." ~ Mahatma Gandhi

# CHAPTER FIVE

# Step Five

## WHAT DO YOU WANT FROM LIFE?

I n my two decades of work, I've found that people desire growth and change, often seeking it promptly. When I reflect on life in general, it seems that as a human society, we have come a long way, and now, the demand for immediate gratification has overshadowed almost everything else.

We all aspire to achieve greatness and strive to be the best versions of ourselves. Life's challenges often propel us through pain toward achieving something significant, yet we rarely grasp this initially. These challenges exist to foster our growth. However, amid life's struggles, we sometimes lose sight of our strengths, talents, and inherent creativity within us. Many of us live in fear rather than security, especially in times of constant change where uncertainty looms over our job security, income, and housing. At times, we become so fixated on the future that we neglect the present moment. Our vulnerability can keep us stuck, leading us to question: What do I truly want from life?

The daily grind of nine-to-five work can weigh us down, fostering competitiveness as a means of survival. Sometimes, we even place blame on others for our failures and problems. In moments of despair, hope may seem elusive, but it's crucial to recognise that every challenge is an opportunity for growth.

In recent years, there has been a growing awareness of work-life balance, shedding light on the stresses and anxieties we face. Achieving balance is possible, yet the more we focus on life's anxieties, the more it can exhaust our mind, body, and soul. What do I want from life? Is it a fulfilling career, a larger home, happiness, a family, harmonious relationships, love, or healing from past wounds? These are questions worth pondering as we navigate our journey.

Since we live in the third-dimensional reality and rely on our five senses, it's easy to think that's all there is. However, I can assure you there is much more beyond this. Our senses have expanded, our evolution has progressed, and we've witnessed higher intuitive growth in recent years.

We inhabit a body, which serves as our shell and physical vehicle.

Our mind facilitates learning and the absorption of knowledge and information.

The heart connects us deeply to others and fosters relationships, bringing joy and profound fulfilment.

The soul seeks peace, inner fulfilment, clarity, and higher connections, constantly evolving.

If we ask ourselves what we want from life, numerous answers may surface as we rationalise and prioritise our desires.

Throughout my life, I've experienced both small and significant successes, driven by my efforts and determination. People often inquire about my achievements and the source of my energy, describing me as a whirlwind.

It's important to acknowledge that every accomplishment requires effort and time. As someone who strives to achieve, I've confronted numerous traumatic challenges that have tested my resilience. These trials could have either made or broken me, and I chose to grow stronger. Inner strength and resilience, I believe, have propelled me from one success to the next.

Some have remarked that I possess a gift that must be shared with the world, a sentiment I accept. As Paula once told me, "You wouldn't be given anything you couldn't handle."

Inspiring others has always been my passion. During my time as a mentor in schools, I developed action plans to help children discover their best selves. Emotionally, I aimed to bring smiles to their faces and foster happiness. Mentally, I strived to create safe and peaceful environments. Physically, I encouraged their well-being and happiness.

Working closely with children, I learned to appreciate their resilience and sensitivity to the world around them. Together, we set goals and addressed various aspects of their well-being, nurturing their growth in a supportive environment.

## Relationships

Let's delve into the importance of our relationships—whether with family members or our children. In today's era, parents often have limited rights to discipline their children. This brings us to the question: how much freedom should we grant our children? Drawing wisdom from our ancestors and integrating it into our modern world is invaluable. We shouldn't discard the lessons learned from our parents; applying them can benefit future generations, especially our children. It's crucial to maintain some level of parental guidance rather than allowing children to dictate terms. Heart-to-heart conversations can open up discussions on sensitive topics within families, aiming for a balanced approach rather than rebellion. We aim to prevent unnecessary arguments and find common ground between differing viewpoints.

Instilling morals into our societies holds significant value. When my children were growing up, our family dinners were a cherished time. During meal preparations, eating, and afterward, we devoted time to educating ourselves about the world. Every dinner was purposeful, engaging, and memorable, using various methods to enhance our learning and bond as a family. Don't you agree that discussing our world during dinner with loved ones is precious?

Mentoring has been my passion for decades, whether bringing smiles, imparting knowledge, or teaching about mind, body, and soul. Personal growth and empowerment hinge on what we, as adults, display and teach our children. As elders, guiding our family members wisely sets an example for generations to come. Transforming our own well-being and lives influences those who follow us; setting a positive example should be our aim.

Life isn't a mere game; serious challenges arise. However, amid challenges, finding joy and fun is crucial. Life resembles a game of Snakes and Ladders; we choose to progress, stay stagnant, or even regress. If given the choice, what "game" would you play in life? Is it about progressing, releasing anxieties, or both? My life experiences, filled with challenges and traumas, reveal the resilience needed to navigate life's twists and turns. Life's seriousness doesn't diminish its preciousness.

Remarkable events have unfolded in my life, often leaving me in awe, wondering how they came to pass. Heightened awareness illuminated these unique moments, revealing deeper insights and solutions to life's challenges. Enhanced awareness fortifies the whole person—mind, body, and soul—in confronting life's trials.

## Setting Intentions

Setting intentions and goals to get what we want is a process. Intentions should not be fleeting but consistent.

Getting resolutions for growth is something we might think about. How many of us break our New Year's resolutions? Most people do unless they are really determined. It's almost like when you see a bar of chocolate in a shop and the temptation is there. The willpower is probably weak, so you may end up buying the chocolate and eating it all in one go. Hence, the diet has literally gone out of the window. Willpower and determination to achieve resolutions are not always easy for many people.

Our intentions or resolutions should be stronger. There may be some ancestral baggage of lack of determination, willpower, and the intention to change.

Let's take a closer look at the determination of intentions. Intentions are what we pay attention to when we act. They are an action plan. What do we want to do? What is the goal? For example, if you're intentionally looking for a job, you'll set out to look for one. You'd look on websites and in newspapers, wherever that may be. The intention is to make it a habit. Intention is like a landmark, a compass that guides you from one place to another. Intention can be like planting a seed, watering it, and seeing how it grows. So, we have to be careful to cultivate positive habits, and then we'll see the blossoming flower.

Your intention is your path, your desired path, and when you take action, you're on a purposeful path. It will take you from one place to another. Every small intentional action takes you to a bigger place, which is the goal. Having clear intentions can help make life meaningful. Every intention is your goal to make it a purpose. The road ahead is your roadmap to a desired destination.

When you wake up in the morning, you may have some sense of purpose for the day, and you look to fulfil it. You fulfil it because you realise it's a clear intention and it empowers you to create the most meaningful experiences. Meaningful intentions are when you're looking for something and want to put it into action. You will do everything in your power to seek and realise it. Intention will help you take the action to make a change. These are parts of your positive habits that will help you flourish.

Remember that your intention is like a compass that shows you the way. Intentional thoughts are like a seed that you plant. You nurture it, and it grows. Can you see that seed becoming a flower because you have nurtured it—metaphorically speaking—and you have seen that seed grow and blossom into something absolutely beautiful? This is the miracle of you; your intention is your path, your desired path.

## What Is Your Goal?

What is a goal or a destination? It's something we truly desire, something we want to work toward. We try hard because we are determined to achieve it. It's like footballers who train hard every day. They have a goal in mind, a target they are focused on. They think about how they can score another goal, so they train hard because they know that's how they can prepare for it. They have a team, and they put a plan into action. They visualise it, they dream it, they know it, they want it, and then they know the goal is within reach. They pursue it because it is their ambition. Every single player has a goal in mind, driven by their own motivation, and this drives them to act. The same principle applies in every company. You see yourself taking action through your own determination and effort. Isn't this a great concept?

You can apply this same idea to your life. If you want to be the next best hairdresser, dream of having your own store with your staff as team players, and bringing in customers—a goal achieved. Then, your motivation to attract even more customers increases. You have studied hard to qualify, and now it's time to apply it.

Sheer determination and effort will drive individual achievement. Now, let's take this same thought but in a different scenario. A couple contemplates getting married; they fall in love but are unsure if they should marry sooner or later, as it is a new relationship. They communicate and share their thoughts. They have the goal of getting married, but there is so much at stake: happiness, whether it will work out, the cost of the wedding, the organisation, and the stress involved. After a heart-to-heart talk, they decide to take the steps. They spend months working and organizing it. They are motivated and put in the effort. It was not easy, but the ambition and aspiration were there to make it happen. They achieved their goal.

Determination assists you in reaching your goal, fuelled by the emotional connection and drive of your aspirations. Achievements are tasks accomplished, and when we put our minds to getting what we want, it is achievable. I believe mind maps help you rationalise what's important and navigate the various elements you are looking for.

Goals take time and effort to achieve; they do not happen overnight. The intention to achieve something and the desire to pursue the goal make it attainable. Motivation and perseverance are key. Below are seven steps to assist you with your goal.

## Below are seven steps to assist you with your goal.

1. Determine what you want from life

2. Get the clarity and don't get confused

3. You may see the goal as impossible, don't let the fear stop you

4. Make a mind map of what you want

5. Keep motivated

6. Persevere

7. Celebrate the outcome

Now that you are progressing through the knowledge and understanding, please take action on the above steps. Remember, your path is important, whether it is big or small, to get to where you want to be.

Take time to reflect at this point before you move on to the next chapter.

Okay, ready? Let's go!

"When obstacles arise, you change your direction to reach your goal; you do not change your decision to get there." ~ *Zig Ziglar*

CHAPTER SIX

# Step Six

## AWARENESS AND SELF-REFLECTION

A wareness is what is happening to you right now as you have read and thought about some of the ideas given. At this stage, you have applied some of the techniques, if not all, to assist your personal growth. I have used all of these techniques and I wanted to bring awareness to you.

I wondered what life was all about and why my extreme challenges of growing up into adulthood were such a test. Growing up without a father figure, in fact, my mother was both father and mother as I mentally accepted that thought. I also had an awareness when things were going to happen before they happened. I felt that was my sixth sense. Remember when I said I felt there was more than just the third-dimensional space? I meant that we have the capability to tap into more awareness as we progress in life. I use these words: THE WORLD IS YOUR OYSTER / ANYTHING IS POSSIBLE.

Through my own experiences, I know that I have manifested things, people, situations, global speaking events, and much more. I have also taught these techniques to my groups.

It started more consciously, I would say, when I became disabled for the second time and lay on my sofa barely able to breathe due to breathing difficulties. I closed my eyes and started getting insights. I could see a convertible car, and it would be mine. Even though I was struggling so much with my health, I knew I had to survive this health problem. I had to recover; I could not remain disabled. Not long after, this car was in my driveway.

Awareness about life itself is something we may have thought about more as we got older. It seems like the younger years of adolescence are a time to enjoy life and think less, with less awareness of what is happening.

Awareness is a state where we become conscious of what is happening around us, whether it's something that affects us directly or pertains to our environment. In this state, we begin to understand more and become increasingly aware of the events unfolding around us. Through our consciousness, we accumulate experiences, which shape us. The more aware we become, the better equipped we are to help ourselves.

Certainly, I've noticed a significant difference in the past decade, with more people becoming aware. The younger generations, however, might not be fully aware of things yet because they are on their own paths, learning from their ups and downs, and experiencing life. They will grow from their own successes and mistakes, which they might not always be aware of. But as we get older, we become wiser and more aware of the situations around us. We begin to understand why things happen and how to deal with them.

When we find ourselves in a particular situation, our awareness allows us to perceive and understand what is happening. We take in the information, analyse it, and then act and behave in a certain way because we are more aware of what is going on in that situation.

## 3 Levels of Awareness

1. Perception is the awareness of touch, sight, smell, taste, and sound. By using our five senses, we interpret what is happening in our surroundings. Additionally, we can utilize our intuition to receive knowledge without relying on reasoning. Intuition represents an inner knowing, and when combined with perception, they complement each other well.

2. Comprehension refers to how we understand information. We can comprehend things in various ways and from different points of view.

3. Projection involves anticipating what will happen next, including the subsequent steps and the development of awareness and understanding. It pertains to how we utilize this information and what actions we take based on it.

With awareness, our focus sharpens on the information available to us. When navigating through situations, we often draw on our memories, which are linked to our past experiences. It's essential to reflect on these experiences to determine their relevance in the present moment. Making decisions with awareness enhances our wisdom and expands our range of choices. When we are mindful, we begin to select and act upon what we believe is suitable for the circumstances at hand. In doing so, we remain vigilant, assessing potential risks and identifying the tools necessary to navigate the path ahead.

Our self-awareness enables us to empathise with others' feelings and thoughts. When we are self-aware, we make better choices because we understand potential consequences. It allows us to be more attuned to our surroundings, assess our strengths, and reflect on past challenges to decide on better paths forward. Self-awareness is crucial for enhancing relationships, both in professional and personal settings.

Reflection contributes positively to our overall well-being. Daily reflection can be particularly beneficial as it allows us to review our actions and achievements. Through reflection, we can analyse our experiences and consider ways to improve ourselves.

Therefore, growth and self-reflection hold significant value in personal development.

There are various effective methods to engage in self-reflection.

Everyone is different. One way is to find a quiet space where you won't be disturbed. It could be on a park bench, going for a walk or a jog, or simply sitting on your sofa at home in a quiet area.

Direct your awareness to the day you've just experienced. Ask yourself questions like: How did today go? Did I achieve what I wanted? How were my actions and reactions? Did I prioritise effectively? Did I show kindness?

How often do we sit quietly, in a contemplative or self-reflective mood? Consider how you feel about yourself—your self-worth. Do you appreciate who you are? How do others make you feel? What are you learning on this journey?

Everyone's emotions are valid because they are unique to them. Through reflection, you can achieve a balance and better understanding of your own emotions and those of others.

Regular self-reflection helps you recognise your strengths, skills, and wisdom, as well as areas where you can continue to grow. Another aspect of self-reflection involves writing down thoughts. Many people journal to jot down their feelings and thoughts, sometimes including positive affirmations for the day. Self-reflection allows us to find a quiet space, close our eyes, and let go of the day's thoughts, particularly during the final moments of reflection. This practice is akin to mindfulness or meditation, bringing peace to the mind at the end of the day.

Reflecting on the day's events is also beneficial. It allows you to examine patterns you may like or dislike and identify areas for change. However, it's important not to be overly self-critical, as this can lead to low moods and diminished confidence. Instead, focus on recognizing patterns and the progress you aim to achieve, observing how you are evolving.

## Building Healthy Habits and Routines

What are healthy habits? Resting, getting adequate sleep to function, exercising, connecting with nature, eating nutritious foods, and practicing meditation or finding moments of silence each day.

Resting is crucial for recovery, especially during times of low mood, anxiety, or depression. Our body, mind, and soul often feel exhausted during mental health crises. I've always advocated for 8 hours of sleep to rejuvenate our cells. Adequate sleep enhances our daily functioning. Society is increasingly emphasising exercise, with numerous gyms and programs available. Regular movement is essential to prevent muscle atrophy and weight gain. Exercise releases endorphins and dopamine, boosting our mood and reducing anxiety and stress. Initiatives supporting mental health are invaluable, encouraging individuals to help themselves and promoting overall well-being.

Stepping into nature provides a breath of fresh air, benefiting us emotionally, mentally, and physically. Personally, I've always cherished nature; its absence affects my well-being noticeably. Exposure to natural sunlight provides essential vitamin D, and it's free—just step outside, regardless of the weather. We also need to assess our eating habits—are we consuming enough fresh fruits, vegetables, and salads daily? Global price increases may limit access to these items, depending on individual income. It's important, whenever possible, to prioritise nutritious foods.

Meditation is excellent for calming the mind amid busyness. Even taking 2 minutes daily to quiet the mind can enhance productivity and focus throughout the day.

We have 24 hours in a day, so consider where your hours are spent. Take time to review your day and evaluate your priorities. Think about your healthy habits and how important they are for your overall well-being. The above guidance is here to support you. Today, we will keep it simple and brief on this subject, as many people already know what they should and shouldn't be doing. Below are some actions you can take.

*"Healthy Habits Are The Healthy Outcomes."- Parveen Smith, Transformative Coach*

You have learned more on awareness and self-reflection in this chapter. Applying the steps in each chapter will support your personal growth.

**Here are some actions you can take to support your path to empowerment**

· *Reflection of the day- sit quietly and go through the day's events in your mind.*

1. Take a walk and reflect on your day

2. Ask yourself: how did today go?

3. Ask yourself: did I achieve what I wanted from today?

4. Ask yourself: did I prioritise my actions?

5. Ask yourself: do I VALUE who I am?

6. Ask yourself: how do other people make me feel?

7. Ask yourself: am I learning on this path?

## **Testimonial**

I went through a transformational experience; the session opened my eyes to all the areas that needed balance. As a disabled person I have managed and I was using two walking sticks when I first met Parveen. I was determined to use one, which I have been now. Mentally I have a much clearer mind, my focus is fine tuned. My swallowing and leftover trauma from a very bad run in with Covid have been greatly helped. I'm not usually a hard "No" answer person, when asked to do something like this, I'm a let's try and see if this works, I may choke or I might not! (guess what I haven't been.) This has been the singularly most empowering gift ever given to me by a dear friend Sophia.

The following sessions were a gift also but to myself.

I would say to anyone asking should they try it, Yes, it's as simple as that -

Please it will be the best gift you ever give yourself.
*Paulette Hallam*

*"The goal is not to be better than the other man, but your previous self". Dalai Lama*

# CHAPTER SEVEN

# Step Seven

## EMBRACING CHANGE AND ADAPTABILITY

C hange is not simple for many people. It can be quite disruptive for many. To make changes one must really want to improve on something or themselves.

### Embracing Change

Embracing means being willing to do so—comfortably wanting and welcoming something. When you embrace change, you are ready for something new, ready to transform. You are accepting people, thoughts, feelings, or even ideas. You are now prepared for situations to change. Consider different types of circumstances that could bring you happiness, hope, love, affection, money, business—whatever it may be. This is what change is.

Fear will stop you from embracing change because it keeps you stuck, acting as a barrier, like a brick wall. It holds you back, and no matter what you do, if you are not resilient enough, you will stay stuck rather than breaking down each brick for your own personal growth. Letting go is something people also fear because fear holds you back. This is why this book is all about growth. Too many people stay stuck, finding comfort in the same place. Comfortable seems OK and easy.

What we are teaching you here is to face that fear. Grow, expel the comfort zone, and seek other opportunities for your growth. Imagine not resisting and moving forward without fear. Growth does not lie in your comfort zone. No, it doesn't. It is out there, where you must take steps along the path to grow. It may seem uncomfortable because change is uncomfortable for some people. When you are ready to change and embrace it, you will feel exhilarated. Opportunities can be bountiful.

Embrace change and be flexible, almost like a meandering river. Change is good. Staying stuck is stagnant. When you are stagnant, it will be like a murky pond with still waters—you are not flowing. So, keep embracing change. If I can encourage you to do this, anything is possible. To be resilient in growth, you have to take the steps out of your comfort zone to make it happen.

Surely all who are reading this book want to grow both professionally and personally? Sometimes, to take that path, we have to let go of things that are comfortable. You will need a strong positive attitude to take those steps forward, even though it may feel like you're stepping through muddy waters. Those muddy waters can be helpful because one day you will realise how stuck you were. I speak from personal experience—I was stuck and didn't know how to get out. Eventually, I found my answer and knew I had to break free, which I did.

Who said life was easy? Is it time for a cup of tea? In England, we say, "Everything will be alright after a nice cup of tea." I would say it helps.

Human beings are powerful, and we can get through difficult challenges with support. This is why people meet to chat over a cup of tea or coffee to lessen their worries. A friend or colleague may suggest changes to support your journey.

Every powerful, successful person has walked a hard path to achieve growth. You've made a decision, you've been positive, you're taking action, and you are willing to take the positive risk for growth. The more you take this risk, the stronger you will become, and your mindset will change with each step. It's all about where you want to go and how much you want to progress and embrace change.

In the last two decades, I have helped many people transform their lives. I see many who come to me wanting to change but are stuck in their comfort zones. Some have been stagnant for so long that it has made them unhappy, leading to low moods, stress, anxiety attacks, and even depression. Some of my clients have ended up in the hospital due to anxiety attacks because they didn't know how to get help. They hadn't received the support they needed to embrace change.

Many people have stayed stuck in their professional careers or businesses for decades because they thought it was the normal thing to do. They didn't know what lay on the other side of the depressive path, so they went with that flow. The same can be true for relationships; some people stay in the same relationship because they fear what else is out there for them.

Unhappiness is a form of illness, encompassing low mood, sadness, anxiety, and stress. Embracing change offers many opportunities and possibilities, drastically altering your situations and circumstances.

I was talking to Dave, and he shared this with me:

I began my coaching journey before I even realised it. My early years were spent as a sports coach; at the tender age of 13, I was already assisting with coaching the under-6s at my rugby club. While some might say they stumbled into coaching, my path was more deliberate. My mother, my hero whom I lost at 21 and who battled severe illness throughout my teens, was the cornerstone of her friends' circle, offering advice, support, and help. I witnessed firsthand how conversations in her presence could shift from tears to relief and finally to smiles. That experience profoundly influenced me.

What Dave shares here highlights the influence of positivity and the power of embracing change even during challenging times. I love how these examples show us how much we can grow with adaptability.

Sometimes, I have clients who come to me after being in abusive relationships. They have been stuck in so many abusive situations that they didn't know any different or how to get out of it, so they stayed. They thought there was no other way to change. Eventually, they became sick and somehow escaped their relationship. They may have waited six months or even a year. Their initial contact with me was to make that change.

They often say, "I wish I had done this sooner," because their anxiety and depression had worsened, leading to increased medication. They became dependent on medication rather than looking at changing their situation. While medication may still be necessary, the core problem was that they didn't know how to change things. We fully understand that the root of the problem was fear—intense, paralysing fear that doesn't want you to change the situation.

Imagine you've just left an abusive relationship. Now you're living on your own, trying to make ends meet. You go to work feeling low and depressed, but you continue because the job pays the bills. Yet, the unhappiness, sadness, and pain are deep within. How many years has that hurt been inside your soul, mind, emotions, and body?

In this situation, a person came to see me. After a phone call, we decided it was time for a change. This person was willing to do anything to get out of the depression and to consider how a future relationship with a new partner could be better—more in tune and in alignment. The trauma of the past hurt they carried was still there. The only way to change was to embrace it and make the change to release the hurt and trauma. As painful as it would be, this was the only way forward.

By embracing the change with support, this person could deal with things much better after the wellness sessions. They gained clarity and the strength to stand up to situations, feeling lighter mentally and emotionally.

Imagine if I hadn't taken the steps to change my life and my world. I would have definitely stayed stagnant, locked in fear, anxiety, stress, and even depression. Decades ago, I decided to change my life because I wanted to be the best person I possibly could be. The change needed to happen for me and my family. As I embraced the change, I took the fear and turned it around. I'm not saying it was easy because fear is really crippling. Don't forget, I lived with it for years.

Sometimes we justify or question what the best way forward is. I knew for a fact I did not want to stay disabled. I knew for a fact that my children and my husband needed me. I couldn't just give up there. I had many epiphany moments—nudges and guidance. If I hadn't listened to them, I would have stayed stagnant for sure. At this point in my life, I realised I was here for a purpose. I went into deep reflection, pondering questions about my own existence.

I came to a point where I reflected on all the paths I had trodden, from the pain, heartache, suffering, tears, sadness, anxiety, and depression. My mind was curious and needed to explore more because I started to believe there was more. During this time, seeds were sown for my own growth. My curiosity about my life led me to go deeper.

I didn't stop having fun; I enjoyed every part of life. Life became even more precious. Embracing change, as I share with you, is part of the transformative path.

## Adaptability

When new situations come into our lives, we adjust. New situations, new spaces, new environments, new people—we learn to be more flexible rather than rigid. We want to grow, so we look for different things to put into place. We take action in various ways because we become more open-minded. When we seek growth, we find different ways to adapt.

Let's say we face a challenge; we may need to change our course, our path, or our approach, and we may have to look for ways to adapt. We all have the ability to do that. We have a choice within our own space or with people, friends, or relationships regarding what we want and what we do not want. We may see clearly who can easily adapt and who finds it hard. When you are motivated to get something done, you will easily adapt to the situation for the best outcome. Easy-going people can adapt their sense of humour to the mood of the space and even change their behaviour. Adapt to the environment, adapt to the crowd, and learn from that.

For example, if we're playing a board game, we may adapt our strategy to win. Who doesn't want to win? People in business and company leaders learn to adapt quickly because it involves critical thinking, solving problems, and being creative. One key aspect of adaptability is doing it all with calmness. Without calmness, we cannot adapt swiftly. One of the most valuable skills of adaptability is to look at your personal and professional growth, seeing what changes you will allow within your sphere.

Adaptability is all about change; it is about flexibility. Adaptability is also the journey.

We've already looked at how adapting can be difficult for some people because we get used to the same old routines and sometimes don't look outside the box. But if you can imagine how much greater life can be by adapting, rather than feeling restricted, it makes a big difference.

You may be reading this and thinking, "I don't need to adapt, I don't need to change," and you may well be happy exactly where you are, and that's fine too. But for some of you reading this, ponder upon some of the things you may have wanted to do but didn't. Think about the opportunities you may have missed because you didn't like change or didn't want to adapt.

Imagine a person who doesn't like flying and is scared of it. They would be missing out on the beauty of our world, on opportunities, cultures, people, and food. They would miss out on experiences. I know people who have lived like this and have not experienced a world outside their own town. Due to fear and not receiving help, they missed traveling outside their comfort zone.

We all have choices, and we are capable of making choices that serve our highest good. However, when it comes to opportunities and not adapting or resisting change, many opportunities can be missed. Reflecting on my ancestors, I can say that with the little they had, they embraced opportunities, adapted, and explored the world around them. I am deeply grateful for their resilience, which I believe is inherited within myself.

Curiously, we can consider how children cope with change. Children adapt quickly as they learn to listen and follow instructions, often for their own benefit—such as behaving well to receive a reward. They exhibit changing behaviours to align with what they believe they deserve. Children continuously adapt from nursery to preschool, primary school to secondary school, and later to college or university. These transitions can be challenging for children, but as adults who have been through it, we encourage them to be the best they can be and support them to the best of our abilities.

I personally believe we should encourage children to adapt with loving and caring guidance from parents. This approach helps them feel more secure and nurtured in life. As discussed earlier, sometimes we choose not to follow in our own parents' footsteps due to difficult past experiences or less-than-ideal upbringing. This is why as adults; we must initiate change and adaptability to pave the way for future generations.

Let's acknowledge the efforts we've made to bring about this change and adaptability for our children's future. We deserve a pat on the back for the positive impact we're creating.

Like a butterfly undergoing metamorphosis from a caterpillar, we too must embrace change. I often tell my students that change is inevitable; we must continue to evolve. What worked two years ago may not work today, so it's crucial to move with the times, embrace the new, and adapt—for our own sake and for the benefit of future generations.

## Cultivating Resilience and Mindfulness

Resilience encompasses enduring hardships, facing life difficulties, and sometimes encountering traumatic experiences. It manifests in various forms, defined by the capacity to rebound from adversity. Resilience is fundamentally the ability to recover from challenging situations, adapting effectively in the face of adversity, trauma, tragedy, threats, or significant stressors. Resilient individuals navigate life's highs and lows with resilience, maintaining a positive perspective and functioning effectively despite adversity. Developing resilience entails fostering coping skills, problem-solving abilities, strong social support systems, and finding purpose or meaning in life. This quality is crucial for navigating tough times and emerging stronger from them.

Cultivating resilience is crucial for maintaining mental health and well-being. Resilience involves the capacity to adapt and recover from tough situations. Building strong social connections and support networks is a key strategy to foster resilience. Surrounding yourself with family and friends who offer emotional support can significantly aid in navigating challenging times. Personally, I'm fortunate to have a supportive family, which has made a profound difference in my life. Building and nurturing a supportive social circle is equally invaluable.

Moreover, incorporating self-care practices and maintaining a healthy lifestyle, which includes regular exercise, proper nutrition, and sufficient sleep, further enhances resilience. Participating in activities that bring joy and relaxation, like hobbies or mindfulness practices, is also beneficial for managing stress and cultivating emotional resilience.

It's crucial to develop problem-solving skills and cultivate positive thinking patterns. Learning to reframe negative thoughts and concentrate on finding solutions can significantly improve your ability to navigate challenges effectively.

Finally, seeking support from me and my practitioners can empower your journey. We offer additional tools and strategies for building resilience through techniques that aid in processing difficult emotions, developing coping skills, and fostering a stronger sense of self-awareness and self-efficacy.

So, when I meet people and they ask, "How did you get through that? How can you keep smiling?" It's because they can sense the essence of who I truly am. The individuals I've encountered along my journey can perceive my soul-level essence.

It is the same within this book. I am grateful for being alive, healthy and well now. I am an innovator of wellbeing. So many techniques have already been mentioned within this book. These tools have consistently supported me in navigating life's challenges, of course life gets in the way too, we may not follow them all the time but they've always been there for me to fall back onto.

I met a lady at a conference, after listening to my story of trials and tribulations she said this is something like out of EastEnders. The whole group laughed. So, I speak about trials and tribulations of life and stress and traumas because I don't think we should feel ashamed of them.

A lot of people I meet bury the traumas, bury the heartache, the sadness because they find it difficult. After they have conversed with me, they realise the unhealthy side, and want my support to assist their healing process.

One thing we shouldn't do is feel ashamed of ourselves. Life presents us with scenarios and situations to experience and grow from, all of which deserve our respect. Consider where you are today—you've made it this far, so give yourself a pat on the back.

To maintain a positive self-perception, it's crucial to be mindful of our thoughts and how we perceive ourselves. Avoid self-criticism and instead, treat yourself with kindness and encouragement. Every emotional thought we have about ourselves matters; negative thoughts can lead to negative outcomes. Instead, focus on seeing yourself as capable and doing absolutely fabulous.

The more we cultivate an internal view of ourselves as loving and caring individuals, projecting that intention outwardly, the more it influences our external behaviour. As we elevate our perceptions of ourselves, we also enhance how we perceive others and interact with them.

Everyone possesses unique personalities, characteristics, habits, and attitudes. Our differences don't prevent us from getting along; rather, they enrich our interactions. By communicating thoughtfully and mindfully, we gain deeper insights into others' perspectives and behaviours. This understanding fosters harmonious relationships and allows us to connect effectively with anyone.

I often notice that many people struggle to get along with others, which may be due to their inherent traits and characteristics. These traits could have been passed down from their ancestors. For instance, if someone often appears gloomy and downcast, and you've observed a parent with the same demeanour, it might be an inherited trait. This observation comes from being interested in people. Observing people is something I enjoy, and it's not uncommon to notice that the habits of parents and their children are strikingly similar, leading to the conclusion that many qualities and characteristics are inherited.

## Nurturing Relationships and Connections

Nurturing yourself is the first part of nurturing any relationship, if one cannot nurture themselves how will they be able to nurture their loved ones. Having healthy caring relationships whether with friends or colleagues comes to our self-care and acceptance first.

This also ties into the question of the best way to raise our children in this world. We can nurture our children and give them gifts; we might even spoil them with an abundance of toys or new games. However, I perceive a problem in this approach if they are given gifts too regularly. I say this because as they grow older, they may not appreciate the value of things and could develop an expectation of receiving from others.

Communicating, nurturing children with unconditional love, recognising their innocence, and appreciating the way they express love to their parents can have a profound impact. This approach is unconditional and does not require monetary value or anything in return. I taught my children these values. I also know that not all parents can afford gifts or spoil their children. The unconditional loving communication is priceless.

Nurturing relationships is about delving deeper; it involves taking responsibility for your family members, particularly the young ones. Guiding your children now will assist their emotional and mental wellbeing.

Parents often face these dilemmas: what's the best approach to raise children? Refraining from giving treats might be seen as mean; while taking away privileges can be perceived as emotional blackmail by the child. These challenges highlight the complexities of modern-day parenting.

Twenty or thirty years ago, parents had more leeway in disciplining their children. With changes in laws and societal norms, discipline has seemingly diminished. Today, I often hear parents asking how to raise children in our current culture, where there's a prevalent blame culture. This concern has been voiced repeatedly over the years, and it continues to be a topic of discussion.

When we endeavour to nurture our children and those around us, we are aware that various influences can sway them from their intended path. Our natural inclination is to nurture them and guide them back to a safe space because of our care and love for them, wanting only the best.

I also know in the days that we live in now it's really difficult for some parents. Hence then the extra support is needed. During any difficult period, it is still the same as we should still teach our children as much respect as possible.

We understand that when we nurture our children and those around us, various influences may lead them astray. Generally, we guide them back to safety because we care for and love them, hoping only the best for their well-being.

In today's challenging times, parenting can be particularly tough, additional support is required for parents who struggle. Likewise, I would say for the children. Even during these difficult periods, it remains crucial to teach as much respect in our children as possible. I personally feel the emotional connection with the child is paramount.

I feel every parent has a responsibility to teach their children respect and manners and it should not be the responsibility of other sources such as childminders, schools and playgroups as we hear every now and then.

So, if we all take responsibility for those around us that little bit more maybe we will take the pressures of our services. As we know there are a lot more community groups nowadays that bring people together. There are definitely more supportive groups around.

The nurturing comes in whether it's from a friendship and new person they just met. The nurturing can come in place at work, the office and any space in fact.

We probably have seen a big shift in nurturing relationships in the workplace. We are learning to put human beings first; this is due to mental health problems that we have seen escalating over the decades.

In relationships we may see people more independent and some are more interdependent. Some people seem to be ready to get up and go and do anything and accomplish anything. Whereas some people will need extra support and become more interdependent on those around them this could be in the workplace or in personal life. We start to understand the more connections we make with people the better it is.

When a person is anxious, stressed, fearful, depressed or in a low mood they will isolate themselves or become isolated. When we become more aware we can assist them to get the right support. When people become isolated, we can help them and nurture them and build connections with them once again. Clearly it may not be easy but the journey starts to begin.

When we are in nurturing relationships and we build that connection and the friendships develop deeper, we have more hobbies and more gatherings that we can go to together. Social interaction brings empathy and synergy between the people. When we develop these relationships and nurture them and the connections are made there is more of a connection on more than one level mentally, emotionally, and on a soul level.

## The Value Of The Connection Deepens.

So, as we have just looked at relationships with others and our children but what about nurturing our relationships with our loved ones? Nurturing a relationship with our loved one is very important to take time to be together to eat together to be walking together, to go out for meals together. For those of you who have a partner this must not be neglected.

So, as you go on to this transformative path with the seven steps that will empower you for your growth this also involves being mindful and aware of your partner. Even though the path is yours individually and uniquely which is what I would usually say focus on, we don't want to leave our partners too far behind. For your own growth keep growing and encourage your partner to come on the journey with you, adjacent to you. It's always intriguing to see how couples meet and what drew them together to be soulmates. When I see true soul connections, I see them as they have this amazing call within them to meet each other. And I see two souls who are meant to be together forever. They have this amazing connection.

Connecting with your partner is imperative for a long-lasting relationship as we already all know. Some people say they work hard at their relationship and connect with one another whereas others will say we are here for the long run and it's just as it is.

Meeting your partner across a dual carriageway in a city centre just by eyes meeting is what normally people would say love at first sight. And when this relationship lasts 35 years it may have had some ups and downs and that's part of life's trials and tribulations yet the longevity is there. So, I would say the connections and the real talks really do matter keeping that balance of love and harmony.

If you believe in energy and that we all have energy around us and you are energy beings, would you say energy attracts another person to you? I am a strong believer of this. And sometimes people say what a great aura you have. What does that really mean? We can look into this concept because everybody has an energy field, and the energy field attracts or magnetises or repels.

So, this is why we will have a greater connectivity with some people and less of a connectivity with other people. And you may have heard opposites attract too. This is true because one person in the relationship may love to listen to rock music and the other person may love to listen to gentle music. One person in the relationship may love walking and the other person in the relationship may be a hermit. So now you can see how interesting it can be to see opposites attract. They can still have a great connectivity on a soul level and yet their physical world could be slightly different. This can also reveal that this can be a great loving harmonious relationship.

# Below are 7 steps of reminder that can support your journey

1. Change is good. Remain in a flexible mindset.

2. Learn new skills and techniques. Be open to new ideas.

3. Embrace opportunities. Broaden your horizons.

4. Thinking on your toes. Bounce back from setbacks.

5. Manage stress levels. Stay in the present moment.

6. Be open to criticism. It supports your path.

7. Calmness is the beauty of the soul.

"The secret of change is to focus all of your energy not on fighting the old, but on building the new." – *Socrates*

# CHAPTER EIGHT

# Final Thoughts

I realise I
want more
out of life

Power Of Transformation is a Gift of hope. Three things which I work with are Love, Transformation, and The way.

What does all this mean? It is a process of transformation in the wellness sessions which allows deeper change. It is not something that you can reach from the exterior, it is only something that chemicalises from within. So why is nurturing oneself so integral, my answer to that is because without the whole-body system working effectively like a machine it will break down and it may take a long time to fix and even be costly.

This is why our wellness sessions have transformed so many people already. The mentoring, coaching and nurturing brings deeper connections for the body to work in a whole way is the ultimate life source. The game of life is to make it work for you.

## Celebrate Your Success

Celebrating success and continued growth are important to me. I've always marked my achievements, whether with a cheer over a drink, a meal out, or purchasing something of personal value. Worth is subjective; what holds value for one may not for another, and it's up to each of us to define what is meaningful.

Your ongoing growth occurs when you recognise your achievements and strive for more of what brings you happiness. Some individuals are more driven than others, and success hinges on the determination to act. Personally, I've never struggled with motivation, believing life is too short after facing health challenges. I feel every moment should be cherished, as our time in the universe is brief.

Excessive sleep strikes me as time wasted, akin to forming a habit. When our time here ends, we'll rest for an eternity, making meaningful living crucial now. The power of the mind can shape our outcomes; emotions fuel our actions and magnify our focus. Let's channel positivity and motivation to achieve our best selves.

We can stagnate or move forward; I advocate for action. Quiet moments matter, and brief meditation can be beneficial in our pursuit of a fulfilling life. Life offers the best when we actively pursue our desires. Procrastination keeps us stuck; act decisively today to manifest your aspirations. You deserve what you desire most, once you realise how to attain it.

## Embracing Your Transformed Self

1. Journal daily thoughts

2. Sit quietly allow the mind to quieten down

3. Reflect on your day

4. Give yourself praise

5. Enjoy everything you have around you

6. Gratitude is the attitude towards a successful life

7. Remember you are the greatest asset to a transformative path of personal growth and empowerment

I have this next story of Francis who came to me as she was feeling stuck in life, I would say it was mainly her job. She was feeling extremely depressed.

She could barely speak and was unable to smile. Her anxiety levels were so high that she dreaded going into work. The dread seeped through daily, she didn't know what to do and she didn't have anyone to talk to. When she phoned in despair, I will say I knew I had to see her straight away. Hence, we booked the appointment for the next day.

## Below is Francis's testimonial

I contacted Parveen during a difficult period in my life in which I was experiencing increasing anxiety, low mood and was feeling lost in life. We embarked on a series of wellness sessions which taught me to manage my thoughts and feelings again, rebuild my confidence and regain control over my situation. From Parveen's teachings my confidence and esteem has grown, I'm able to problem solve and once again I am embracing life with enthusiasm. These sessions are transformative.
Francis

*"There are many roads to success, but only one sure road to failure; and that is to try to please everyone else." ~ Benjamin Franklin*

Your habitual essence will either shine or hinder your growth. Now isn't that interesting?

The shifts you decide to make whilst you can will accelerate your growth. Staying in one place of life does not assist your path. Staying in one place can be a lonely journey. You may see people you once knew do more and be more because they decided they wanted more.

Doing the same old will keep you in the same old. Whereas learning and growing will give you more. I remember my family saying what is she doing now? All I was doing was the next thing to learn and grow. Most of the time it was to better myself so I could show others how to better themselves.

I was sharing with a lady recently that we sometimes do not see what's happening right in front of us. There was an unhappy situation with three friends they were all bickering. There was a lack of trust through past conversations. The problem here was that one person had to break the trust out of concern. The person did it from their integrity to keep the other person safe. When they found the trust was shared, the relationship started to drift.

When there is a close friendship unit the last thing anyone wants is upset and divide in the group. No matter what was happening there was no resolution.

After speaking to this lady the first time, she called again for coaching. The coaching that I do is not just the average coaching it is more than that. She was so confused that I cleared some things with her. She then understood that immediate close friends don't always listen to each other. I am a strong believer that that is when outside help is required. We as habitual beings get so used to those around us and our environment that we would not take guidance from each other immediately.

This lady was due to go on a holiday and I remember saying if you would like to enjoy your special holiday with your friends, I would seriously consider a wellness session with me first. She agreed and we did just that. To the point I could see instantaneous reactions in the session. She looked brighter. There was much more clarity and focus for this business woman. I expressed things will be much more harmonious and she would have a healthier experience and enjoy her time with her friends. She came back to me days later and said everything was good and you for everything.

We are creatures of habit and change takes time; adjustment takes time. More often than not we would do the same things we have always done. Doing the same things will give you the same results. If you want change, don't do the same things.

For me I am a strong believer that change is inevitable. At some point whether it is a choice of willingly making a change from suffering to wellbeing today or later. For most people when they realise something has to change something will, in some form, there will be change. It doesn't always mean it was exactly what they wanted as it might not have been a focussed change.

I will just share my thoughts again about how more and more people are realising that our childhood played a big part in our lives. Many people have had great childhoods and I know many haven't. Some people may hold on to heavy thoughts of their childhood being disrupted or disruptive. So, what choice would you make to better your life from the past. I use the phrase you don't need to struggle. Because we have options to improve our lives. To have the best of life is by healing the past. Then allow yourself to embrace life. Life is a journey and we were not given a plan at a young age that guaranteed to give us the best.

We have all received education, the education for a greater emotional and mental wellbeing life was not given to us in our earlier days.

The only manual you will receive is on the journey and through transformative life coaching and trainings. Through my teachings you can navigate and master life. Through the learning there will be opportunities. This is why I have always said change is inevitable when you embrace it in this way of learning, experiencing, transforming,

The adventures start because you took the risk, the chance, the opportunity. When change happens the mindset also changes as the embracing of opportunities takes place,

The topic of the book "Transformative Path". speaks for its self, identifying steps one may take to bring about positive change.

On this note as you all know that your journey is very personal. It takes time to get to your desired goal.

Below you will read some more thoughts from professional people who may have faced challenges and took the power into their hands to get through certain aspects of life to be successful.

I also love supporting organisations where possible when my clients have my services. A portion of that money will be used to help men, women and children in war zones, natural disaster zones, feeding hungry people around the world, and getting aid for orphanages. I spoke with Amaka, she helps women and I wanted to ask her some questions about the importance of women's safety and this is what she said.

## What is importance of looking after women's security?

It is extremely important to first of all give security a very broad meaning in discussing women's safety and security, as only then will it paint a complete picture of the myriads of vital issues that makes a woman feel safe, and the importance of having all these various aspects and factors secured.

Given the all-encompassing roles women play, and their unique physiological make up, women carry a lot of burden and wear different hats in their lives that require dedicated care. Also, the prevalence of violence against women and girls even from people in authority or intimate partners means that they are subjected to abuse from persons who should offer protection. Financial security also allows women to have independence and free of having to live with an abuser for financial dependence.

## Why is supporting women your passion?

Growing up as a girl child in Africa meant that you were raised to recognise your future role as a wife, homemaker and mother with expectations to be seen and not heard. Although I was lucky to have been raised by a father who wanted more for his daughters, I still had to deal with this mindset with an ex-partner and his family, and the extremely patriarchal Army where I served as an officer. Each time I rebelled against these traditions and norms, I did it not for me alone, but for other women/girls who did not have the courage or voice to do so. Eventually, I knew I had to create a more structured method to carry on this support and allow others with the same passion to join in the campaign for women.

## What is it that women can do to change their situation?

There is a need for a paradigm shift in the way women see themselves to change their situations. Women need to shift from the "victimhood" persona and take over the narrative of their lives to change their situation. The days of the "damsel in distress" should all be put away and agency put in its place.

**If you could do any more to help women what would that be?**

If I could do more to help, it would be to dedicatedly equip women with the requisite tools to forge the path they want their lives to take and not to wait in the hope that by some luck or providence that life would "happen".

*Amaka Lawton*
Alpha Omega Women Peace Security Foundation

❖

As a psychosomatic doctor with training in trauma therapy and body therapy, I've long been interested in how trauma is stored in the body. I myself had a serious skiing accident 30 years ago that didn't require hospitalization and didn't involve any broken bones. Apart from a large, painful, swollen knee, it left no obvious lasting damage. It wasn't until two years ago, during the Somatic experiencing training, that I realised that I couldn't get out of the shock for 30 years.

You could say I lived a life in "survival mode". I'm leaving out other traumas such as the loss of the lost twin, caesarean section, birth with an overdose of anaesthetic in the mother and other developmental psychological aspects, although that of course plays a role in the processing of the skiing accident, just briefly: my system wasn't able to drain the energy via suitable grounding.

Rather, my system reacted by building up tension. Still a little tighter. Seven years ago, pain began in the right shoulder, after which physiotherapy did not help, followed by years of Rolfing, bioenergetics, osteopathy and finally somatic experiencing training and energetic healing.

I finally came to Parveen through a coincidence in Crete meeting Sophia who recommended me. To the wellness sessions now:

Which structures exactly does the high-energy vibration hit?

I can't say exactly: is it the tissue water? Is it the microtubules? Or does the light energy run through the DNA and transform?

We don't know exactly yet, but the healing works its way from the energetic field into the physical structures; energetically perceived over thousands of kilometres, the body manages to let go more and more, to really calm the state of high alert.

In the last session it came to a state of trance, the body's alchemy seems to start again. Access to higher knowledge was strengthened and becomes magical, like a wound closing with lots of small molecules working together, in miraculous ways.

Connection to the higher self was restored and this also leads to a reorientation and discovery of gravity in the connective tissue and muscles, therefore releasing step by step the tension and helping the body to heal.

It's pleasant to do nothing and at the same time sometimes not so easy for me to not have to do anything, which makes the name wellness session really appropriate.

So, enjoy your healing time with Parveen and may many people be helped by her work.

*Dr Nadja Weinbach*

❖

My name is **Christopher (Chris) King** and I am 74 years old.

After flying training I joined the Hercules Fleet at RAF Lyneham, Wiltshire. I progressed from Co-Pilot to Captain on 36 and 47 Squadrons respectively. I was selected as a Flight Instructor on 242 Operational Conversion Unit (OCU) and during my years as a Flight Instructor implementing significant operational safety changes to the aircraft handling techniques. During my tour I attended the Central Flying School for 6 months and became a Qualified Flying Instructor (QFI).

A 2-year ground tour at the Royal Air Force College Cranwell followed during which time I trained young and old male and female recruits, both civilian and military, in the fine arts of being an Officer in Her Majesty's Royal Air Force. A welcome return to flying followed on No.32 (the Royal) Squadron. As a senior flying instructor, I added to my duties the role of personal pilot to the Air Officer Commanding the RAF and was his personal pilot during the run-up to Gulf War I visiting many airfields in the Saudi Arabian theatre of War. After 94 days I was returned to base to convert to fly the Lockheed L1011 TriStar aircraft and become, once more, a Transport and Air-to-Air Refuelling pilot with No. 216 Squadron based at RAF Brize Norton. Many hours were spent, both day and night, providing a reliable and constant refuelling platform for the many Royal Air Force Fighter aircraft and our American 'cousins' on an 'as required' basis. Air and ground 'close calls' were, thankfully, few and far between. On returning home I was greeted with a failed marriage and I had a nervous breakdown. Thankfully my distant 'guardian angel' was my saviour and she (Elaine), along with the RAF Medical team, cared for me until I was recovered.

There were several High Stress points in my RAF career, all associated with the conflicts that I was deployed to. Never did I once consider 'throwing in the towel', but the accumulative stresses that extended deployments away from home and a failing marriage caused, resulted in my 6-month early release from my Reservist Contract.

The RAF Medical Services were attentive, sympathetic, helpful and helped me tremendously with a program of follow-up psychiatric doctor appointments. My then companion (now wife) helped me tremendously to cope with the recovery of my confidence and self-esteem and we married and have been together since my return from the Gulf War.

I took a job as an Aircraft Flight Data Analyst which was something that I enjoyed doing. Elaine and I subsequently bought the company and we still manage the business (more Elaine than me) and it provides the means to keep our minds active.

I have been a member since 2004 and have been Branch Chairman and County Chairman during my time. I am currently Branch Chairman of one of the oldest branches which Elaine and I keep 'alive' for its historic value.

Along with all of the other 'concepts' that have been revealed to me I look forward to adding to my knowledge and understanding of this most challenging subject.

Without my wife Elaine and Parveen's support I would not be here today. They have seen me through the most difficult times of my life so far with their unconditional support and, dare I say, love, patience and understanding.

My faith in all that has been placed before me has been strengthened by the clear and patient way that both Parveen and Elaine have taken the

time to explain and actively support me when I needed them most and two 'events' have served to fortify my faith and drive my curiosity to know more.

*Chris RAF Retired Pilot*

❖

My name is **Elaine**

After being a mum of three, now all in their forties, once they were all at school, I felt I needed to do more with my life. My friend and I went swimming on a Wednesday, we saw an advert on the notice board saying about a new Royal Air Force Squadron it was going to be a reserve Squadron (part time). We went to the interview and sat the exams and got accepted into the Aeromedical Airborne Evacuation Squadron Nurse.

With months (14) of training we started to fly. One of my flights was going to the top of Norway, an eight-hour flight to pick up two injured army officers who had been in a skiing accident and needed to get back to England for special treatment. The flight was very traumatic. I thought we had lost one man, but we brought him back again. Lots of things happened, on landing we rushed them to the hospital for ongoing treatment. I was just going home when the officer who I saved asked to see me before going into surgery. He thanked me and said, "thank you for getting me home to my mum". Unfortunately, he did not survive in the end, but for the two weeks only he did get to see his mum. This was a very low moment for me. The other officer had life changing injuries but lived.

The highlight of my career was when I received my Royal Air Force Aeromedical flying wings. I am at my best when I am helping others.

Bringing people home to get the treatment they needed was such a huge achievement for me, there were times when I felt helpless and lost in the moment of pressure, but because you know that there will be someone else out there needing your help, you pick yourself up, think positive and move on.

Once out of the forces I joined the Royal British Legion to help look after forces personnel and their families, it was very much needed to set up a line of communication to them all to make sure they were being looked after and given help when needed. I started that line by telephone communication, a link to all members, sometimes my voice was the only one they heard in a week, it is care in the community, very important to keep people in the loop of progression in their life cycle, we all need to feel part of moving forward in life no matter how small, we are all at different stages moving positively forward.

The topics in this book gives you an insight into how we as humans have a need to progress and look after our core and soul, how to keep the body and mind synchronized with the world, how to respect yourself and look after what you have and help guide others with the gift of your knowledge.

I met Parveen at her last book signing event. I have known her for two years and with her help and guidance she has changed my life so much for the better, her care and knowledge are so impressive and easy to follow. The way she guides you with such confidence is amazing. She is truly an angel and I can't thank her enough.

*Elaine King*
Retired Aeromedical Airborne Evacuation Squadron Nurse

*I am so happy you have made it to the end of the book! Transformative Path is a book you can keep forever to assist you on your journey. There are many things covered in the book as it is your journey. I love to keep things simple, as I usually say the only things that are made complicated are by human beings. Life is not easy for most people as there are struggles of life in our society. I know the steps in the Transformative Path have helped myself and my clients. We can take time to review our lives and observe and receive invaluable perspectives. As we observe through a clearer lens, we can make impactful decisions that motivates us.*

*You have learned a little about transformation, anxiety and stress symptoms, depression, empathic and non-empathic people, the soul and the mind, what do you want from life, awareness and self-reflection, embracing change and adaptability, and the power of transformation. This book may also be enlightening to look out for signs within other people who may require support and do not know where to go, you could be the advocate who can shine the light to the Transformative Path.*

*Remember I have had many traumas in my life that could have destroyed everything, I decided NO this is not where I want to stay stuck, I want more, I want to recover and I want to better my life. Because I took action to transform my path the world is my oyster as I am totally supported by The Universe.*

*So, transform your path from broken dry arid ground to a seedling growing into a beautiful flower. Because there is always a ray of light to support your growth on your Transformative Path.*

*I am always here for you!*

Whenever you are ready, here are some more ways we can work together. I help to mentor and coach those who are struggling with anxiety, stress, feeling lost in life, want more from life, live a happier abundant life and much more. The life you deserve is much more than what you think. I guide individuals seeking personal growth and fulfilment to overcome self-limiting beliefs and achieve their goals through strategic wellness coaching, without unnecessary stress or overwhelm.

The wellness sessions, anxiety stress management training programs are all encompassing personal growth and empowerment.

Once you know what you want you will have growth and transformation.

Look Out For The Next Book!

With Love

*Parveen Smith*

Global Speaker/ Mentor / Coach / Trainer

**www.soul2soulwellbeing.com**

*"YOUR HEALTH IS YOUR FIRST FOUNDATION"*
*Steven Bartlett – Diary Of A CEO*

# Sponsorship

## BY ELAINE AND CHRIS KING

We first encountered Parveen during her book launch and signing at Nantwich Bookshop, where she was introducing her second amazing book about her life's journey and self-healing. At that time, I was recovering from a major surgery, and we were eager to leave the house. Having heard about Parveen's story and her books, Chris and I felt an instant connection upon meeting her. We had a lovely conversation with her afterwards, and our bond began. We arranged a meeting to discuss how she could assist me through my traumatic illness. After reading her book, I was convinced that Parveen was the ideal person to help me. A few weeks later, I suffered a stroke and missed my appointment with her. However, I knew it was crucial to see her; I needed her wisdom and healing guidance once more. When I finally met with her, it was astonishing that, after some time, I no longer required my walking stick, and my speech became clearer to others. It was her resolve and trust in her wellness sessions and abilities that saw me through. Parveen also provided immense support to Chris during his emotional struggles following the events. Subsequently, Chris underwent a heart operation and suffered two heart attacks. It became essential for him to receive Parveen's support. We sought her help and joined several of her wellness workshops, where we met others, she had helped too. Her supportive nature made the wellness workshops enjoyable, prompting us to sign up for Anxiety Stress Management Training. Wings of Change Program, Visualisation, Manifestation Growth Program, as well as AOT level 1. This extraordinary woman transformed our lives. I cannot express enough to the readers of this book the profound wisdom and knowledge Parveen possesses, coupled with her dedication and trust in helping others; she is truly inspirational.

We have chosen to sponsor Parveen as a token of gratitude for all she has done for us. Her contributions deserve recognition; they have the power to transform lives, bringing a sense of fulfilment and happiness. With Parveen's support, we find our physical and mental health greatly enriched. Her reliability is unquestionable, and the wellness sessions she has provided have inspired us to support her in her life's journey.

Thank you from the bottom of our hearts for the wellness of body, mind and soul she has brought us.

*Elaine and Chris King*

# Reviews
# Transformative Path

Only someone who has gone through this can bring solace and clarity for every scenario that we explore. There are great tools and the step-by-step process is clearly outlined.
*Antonetta Fernandes*

Powerful stuff, Parveen! The message which is underpinned, I think, is that through paying attention to our health & wellbeing, we can become successful!

You point to it not necessarily being easy, but through determination & self-belief. one can increase in confidence & move forward!
*Angela Belcher*

Absolutely amazing, nice, and simple explanations for beginners. I literally feel like this book has diagnosed how I feel. The struggles of how I feel and not being able to figure out why I feel like this. This book has helped me find out why I felt the way I felt and how to resolve these issues. A very logical, simple, and powerful book.

*Sunny Heer*

Truly inspirational expression, a simple way to put it. It is usually very difficult to write about mind, emotion, heart and soul and yet you explained softly and may the reader be delighted. Congratulations for the book.

*Nirmal Kumar Thapa*

Transformative path is very informative and easy to read and understand. The book helps me to link things that have happened.

*Elaine King*

# Acknowledgments

*I* would like to thank all of my clients who have received my wellness sessions, my training programs and heard my talks globally.

*I want to thank Lyn Harvey my friend of almost twenty years. We have shared many experiences and my friendship with Lyn remains forever.*

# Read More!

## ARE YOU CRAVING FOR MORE OF PARVEEN'S BOOKS?

*H*er previous books are enlightening about her journey and her own insights to the world around her.

# Book Reviews

*Parveen, I really enjoyed reading your new book. Thank you so much for sharing your experiences and journey. You are a true inspiration following your calling and what you truly believe in, when at times it must have been so hard, when so many would have doubted and not believed you. I felt a feeling of pure serenity while reading and could not put it down. You truly have a gift.*
**Kirsty**

*I have finished reading your book. WOW Parveen! I found it incredibly inspiring, you work so hard and always follow your dreams, spinning and manifesting gold out of ordinary threads of life, showing us what is possible when we dare to believe, truly have faith, and let ourselves be guided by the Divine. It must be a difficult and lonely path at times being one at the front, doing all the hard work so others travel more easily, but you are so obviously divinely supported on your path, your story is a beautiful one, and I can't wait to read the next chapter. Thank you for being you. EMMA*

# **Author Bio**

## PARVEEN SMITH

*Parveen Smith is a Global Speaker who is inspirational. She has overcome many physical health challenges and traumas. She has won Prestigious Powerhouse Global Awards 2023 Empowering Women, Health and Wellbeing Champion New York 2024. Her humanitarian support has been her mission all her life, however big or small. Her work in Europe to transform lives teaching techniques has been invaluable.*

*As a trainer, speaker mentor, she has a constant drive to present strength and capabilities to her clients and leaders. In times of crisis, she has supported many people to manage, on all levels for the benefit of improved situations. Her compassion and concern for humanity has been her mission. Parveen*

*Smith is an accomplished speaker. She has a unique talent of connecting with people. Her skills as a speaker and CEO of her own business are admired by many, she has been transforming lives of people Globally. Her emphasis on supporting individuals and businesses to understand anxiety and stress is impressive. She has totally reshaped her future as a mentor, working in schools over 24 years ago, to her humanitarian work. Her mentoring and dedication to advancing the health of others is paramount to her. When she worked in education supporting children with their emotional, mental and personal wellbeing. As a mentor she was honoured to give back quality of time and care to children who felt sad or unheard, to put a smile on their face. She has supported humanity for decades with emotional, mental and physical aspects of trauma and challenges, be it in times of war or natural disasters. Overcoming her own personal traumas and mental, and emotional sufferings she understands human needs. Being consciously aware of the highly demanding need to support leaders and entrepreneurs too. The present daily challenges are what she is passionate about. Changing the human personal story from extreme traumas to survival to resilience. She has been told that she is an asset and is a great connector with people. Bringing joy and wisdom into every person she meets. You may see her as a Global Speaker, an author, award winner, champion for health and wellbeing, connecting people and bringing connections in societies. Her mission is to reshape our future. The future is bright, we just need to see the light. When we look at each human, we may only see a certain aspect of them and Parveen is an advocate of the whole being. The journey she recognises is not the same for all. Therefore, she is constantly asked to speak on global stages.*

# *Parveen Smith*

*Transformative Life Coach // Global Speaker / Trainer / Prestigious Global Award Winner 2023 Health & Wellbeing Champion 2024 New York*

*Soul2Soul Wellbeing*

*http://www.soul2soulwellbeing.com*

## Simply Book Your Transformative Coaching With Parveen

# Review Ask

## LOVE THIS BOOK? DON'T FORGET TO LEAVE A REVIEW!

Every review matters, and it matters a *lot!*
Head over to Amazon or wherever you purchased this book
to leave an honest review for me.
I thank you endlessly.

Thank you for reading my book.

I really appreciate all your feedback and love hearing what you have to say.

I need your input to make the next version of this book and future books better.

Please leave a review on amazon letting me know what you thought of the book.

*Thank You So Much!*

# References

*World Health Organisation*

*Mental Health UK*

*Health & Safety Executive*

*Health Champion*

*Istop4aGP*

*Mind Charity*

# Recommended Reads

*Defining Moments: Coping With the Loss of a Child* - Melanie Warner

*Mom I have a problem: Sophia Manarolis M. Ed*

# ABOUT DEFINING MOMENTS PRESS

B uilt for aspiring authors who are looking to share transformative ideas with others throughout the world, Defining Moments Press offers life coaches, healers, business professionals, and other non-fiction or self-help authors a comprehensive solution to getting their books published without breaking the bank or taking years. Defining Moments Press prides itself on bringing readers and authors together to find tools and solutions.

As an alternative to self-publishing or signing with a major publishing house, we offer full profits to our authors, low-priced author copies, and simple contract terms.

Most authors get stuck trying to navigate the technical end of publishing. The comprehensive publishing services offered by Defining Moments Press mean that your book will be designed by an experienced graphic artist, available in printed, hard copy format, and coded for all ebook readers, including the Kindle, iPad, Nook, and more.

We handle all the technical aspects of your book creation so you can spend more time focusing on your business that makes a difference for other people.

Defining Moments Press founder, publisher, and #1 bestselling author Melanie Warner has over 20 years of experience as a writer, publisher, master life coach, and accomplished entrepreneur.

You can learn more about Warner's innovative approach to self-publishing or take advantage of free training and education at: MyDefiningMoments.com.

## DEFINING MOMENTS BOOK PUBLISHING

If you're like many authors, you have wanted to write a book for a long time, maybe you have even started a book ... but somehow, as hard as you have tried to make your book a priority, other things keep getting in the way.

Some authors have fears about their ability to write or whether anyone will value what they write or buy their book. For others, the challenge is making the time to write their book or having accountability to finish it.

It's not just finding the time and confidence to write that is an obstacle. Most authors get overwhelmed with the logistics of finding an editor, finding a support team, hiring an experienced designer, and figuring out all the technicalities of writing, publishing, marketing, and launching a book.

Others have written a book and might have even published it but did not find a way to make it profitable.

For more information on how to participate in our next Defining Moments Author Training program, visit www.MyDefiningMoments.com

Or

email support@MyDefiningMoments.com

# OTHER #1 BESTSELLING BOOKS

## BY DEFINING MOMENTS ™ PRESS

*Defining Moments: Coping With the Loss of a Child*—MelanieWarner

*Defining Moments SOS: Stories of Survival*—Melanie Warner and Amber Torres

*Write your Bestselling Book in 8 Weeks or Less and Make a Profit—Even if No One Has Ever Heard of You*—Melanie Warner

*Become Brilliant: Roadmap From Fear to Courage*—Shiran Cohen

*Unspoken: Body Language and Human Behavior For Business Success*—Shiran Cohen

*Rise, Fight, Love, Repeat: Ignite Your Morning Fire*—Jeff Wickersham

*Life Mapping: Decoding the Blueprint of Your Soul*—Karen Loenser

*Ravens and Rainbows: A Mother-Daughter Story of Grit, Courage and Love After Death*—L. Grey and Vanessa Lynn

*PivotYou! 6 Powerful Steps to Thriving During Uncertain Times*—Suzanne R. Sibilla

*A Workforce Inspired: Tools to Manage Negativity and Support a Toxic-Free Workplace*—Dolores Neira

*Journey of 1000 Miles: A Musher and His Huskies' Journey on the Century-Old Klondike Trails*—Hank DeBruin and Tanya McCready

*7 Unstoppable Starting Powers: Powerful Strategies for Unparalleled Results From Your First Year as a New Leader*—Olusegun Eleboda

*Bouncing Back From Divorce With Vitality & Purpose: A Strategy For Dads*—Nigel J. Smart, PhD

*Focus on Jesus and Not the Storm: God's Non-negotiables to Christians in America*—Keith Kelley

*Stepping Out, Moving Forward: Songs and Devotions*—Jacqueline O'Neil Kelley

*Time Out for Time In: How Reconnecting With Yourself Can Help You Bond With Your Child in a Busy Word*—Jerry Le

*The Sacred Art of Off Mat Yoga: Whisper of Wisdom Forever*—Shakti Barnhill

*The Beauty of Change: The Fun Way for Women to Turn Pain Into Power & Purpose*—Jean Amor Ramoran

*From No Time to Free Time: 6 Steps to Work/Life Balance for Business Owners*—Christoph Nauer

*Self-Healing for Sexual Abuse Survivors: Tired of Just Surviving, Time to Thrive*—Nickie V. Smith

*Prepared Bible Study Lessons: Weekly Plans for Church Leaders* —John W. Warner

*Frog on a Lily Pad*—Michael Lehre

*How to Effectively Supercharge Your Career as a CEO*—Giorgio Pasqualin

*Rising From Unsustainable: Replacing Automobiles and Rockets*—J.P. Sweeney

*Food—Life's Gift for Healing: Simple, Delicious & Life Saving Whole Food Plant Based Solutions*—Angel and Terry Grier

*Harmonize All of You With All: The Leap Ahead in Self-Development*—Artie Vipperla

*Powerless to Powerful: How to Stop Living in Fear and Start Living Your Life*—Kat Spencer

*Living with Dirty Glasses: How to Clean those Dirty Glasses and Gain a Clearer Perspective Of Your Life*—Leah Montani

*The Road Back to You: Finding Your Way After Losing a Child to Suicide*—Trish Simonson

*Gavin Gone: Turning Pain into Purpose to Create a Legacy*—Rita Gladding

*The Health Nexus: TMJ, Sleep Apnea, and Facial Development, Causations and Treatment*—Robert Perkins DDS

*Samantha Jean's Rainbow Dream: A Young Foster Girl's Adventure into the Colorful World of Fruits & Vegetables*—AJ Autieri-Luciano

*Live Your Truth: An Arab Man's Journey In Finding the Courage to Live His Truth As He Identifies as Gay and Coping with Mental Illness*—David Rabadi

*Unstoppable: A Parent's Survival Guide for Special Education Services with an IEP or 504 Plan*—Raja B. Marhaba

*Please, Excuse My Brave: Overcoming Fear and Living Out Your Purpose*—Anisa Wesley

*Drawing with Purpose: A Sketch Journal*—Rick Alonzo

*NYCoffee: Love Fulfilled in the Little Things*—Craig Lieckfelt

*Good Work: How Gen X and Millennials are the Dream Team for Doing Good When Collaborating*—Erin Kate Whitcomb

*Rescue Me: Guided Self-Healing for First Responders: Conquering Depression, Anxiety, PTSD & Moral Injury*—David Hogan

*TreasuresIn Grief: Discover 7 Spiritual Gifts Hidden in Your Pain*—Lo Anne Mayer

*We Three: Their Beginnings*—Derek Drummond

*Ripping off the Mask*—Joseph Lee

Culture Spin—Kristy Wachter

*Discover Your Inner Leader*—Mamta Goyal

*Grit, Growth and Gumption for Women: Three Keys To Lead Yourself and Others With Confidence*—Tinsley English

*Choosing Your Perfect Tree: Tips from a Landscape Designer* – Laural A Roaldson

Printed in Great Britain
by Amazon

46916236R00069